THE RUBY SLIPPERS OF OZ

THE RUBY SLIPPERS OF OZ

RHYS THOMAS

TALE WEAVER
PUBLISHING

LOS ANGELES

THE MAKING OF THE WIZARD OF OZ, by Aljean Harmetz,
A.A. Knopf, © 1977; THEIR FINEST HOUR,
by Winston Churchill, Houghton Mifflin Co., © 1949
"Hollywood Memories" Nov./Dec. 1988 from THE ALMANAC, Franklin Mint

Roberta Bauman photo courtesy of UPI/Bettmann News Photo
Michael Shaw photo courtesy of Los Angeles Times
Photos and script from The Wizard of Oz courtesy of Turner Entertainment Co.,
© 1939 Loew's Incorporated, Ren. 1966 Metro-Goldwyn-Mayer, Inc.
Photo of Smithsonian Institution's display of shoes
and slipper photo courtesy of the Smithsonian Institution, Division of
Community Life, photographer Jeff Ploskonka
MGM Auction photos courtesy of the estate of David Weisz.

Permission granted to reprint lyrics from "Over the Rainbow" by
E.Y. Harburg courtesy Leo Feist, Inc. © 1938, 1939 (Renewed 1966, 1967)
Metro-Goldwyn-Mayer, Inc. All rights of Leo Feist, Inc. assigned to CBS
Catalogue Partnership. All rights administered by
CBS Feist Catalogue. International copyright secured.

Tale Weaver Publishing wishes to extend special thanks to Mr. Sidney Sheldon.

Cover Design by Wong Design
Cover Airbrush by Hugo Quiroga
Edited by Lia Komaiko
Typesetting by Christine Thompson

Library of Congress Cataloging in Publication Data
89-051070
ISBN 0-942139-09-7

Printed in the United States of America

Tale Weaver Publishing, Inc. Los Angeles, CA 90069

ACKNOWLEDGEMENTS

By attempting a work of this scope and odd nature, I was singularly dependent upon the selfless contributions, advice and criticism of many people. To Irv Letofsky and William K. Knoedelseder, Jr., of the *Los Angeles Times* I owe an immense debt of gratitude. Without their encouragement, this book would not have been written.

My deep thanks are due also to those who generously answered my questions, recalled events and supplied unforeseen help through countless hours of research: to Sherry Weinman, Roger Mayer, Diana Brown, Carl Scheele, Ellen Roney Hughes, Marion Kidd and Susie Battle for getting this project started; to Dan Moldea for his Washington D.C. hospitality; to Jack Haley, Jr., John Wilson, Robert Epstein, Chip Baldoni, Pat Broeske, Kathleen Hendrix, Will Bowden, John Fricke, Aljean Harmetz, Arnold Lipsman, Steve Cox, Bob Tamkin, Ozma Baum Mantele, Garrick Langley, Betty Lasky, Richard and Judy Carroll, Malcolm Willits, Pete Carson, Eddie Fisher, Jane Holcomb, Kathleen Guzman, Eric Alberta, Al DiPardo, John LeBold, Kirk Templeman, Michael Pryor, Bill Thomas and Sheila Mason for all their valuable contributions.

I cannot adequately state my great appreciation to a marvelous circle of friends who have become my ruby slipper family. To Tod Machin, Anthony Landini, Michael Shaw, Philip Samuels, and especially to Roberta Bauman, I am forever grateful for support that never wavered. Further, I wish there was a way to thank Julie Collier for genuine kindness that I will always remember.

I owe a special debt to Sally Nelson Harb, Ron Baron, Dick Weaver and Christine Thompson for bringing this story to life on paper.

Finally, for indispensable criticism, support and friendship during the writing of this book, I am most deeply grateful to P.D. "Roscoe" Hoskins, Clio Bob, my poker pals, family and Michelle. Thank you.

To my mother

TABLE OF CONTENTS

Why have the ruby slippers become Hollywood's equivalent of the Holy Grail? Over the years I have listened to dozens of theories — some sound, some silly. In my experience the consensus would indicate they are the symbol of a beloved movie that touches audiences of all ages... a movie that has been viewed as a family event by over one *billion* people (the most seen movie of all time according to the Guinness Book of Records and other trustworthy sources). Personally I think the slippers are lovely to look at — stylish, colorful and beautifully crafted.

Unfortunately, even though I visited the set in the midst of shooting, I never got to see them. That day Judy Garland was wearing her dressing-room slippers... an oversized pair that were green and very fuzzy. Pretty ugly according to my five-year-old tastes.

In no particular order, I feel the following will have increasing impact on the world of movie memorabilia: The "Rosebud" sled from *Citizen Kane,* Scarlett's gown made of curtains from *Gone With The Wind,* Chaplin's bowler hat and cane, the piano from *Casablanca,* an *original* statue of the *Maltese Falcon,* and so on. I do have a secret wish that I'd like to add to this list: the tin "funnel" hat my father wore in *The Wizard of Oz.* My last dollars would go for that little number.

Jack Haley, Jr.
Los Angeles

The intrigue of the ruby slippers, according to a Munchkin — and there is some charm connected with them, what it is we never knew — is that shoes are an archetype that have been a symbol throughout history — the symbol of authority and liberty. They are a container for the feet which carry us down the journey of Life, as Dorothy went down the Yellow Brick Road. The power of the shoes could have taken her home the first day, but she needed to take the journey down the Yellow Brick Road.

Ozma Baum Mantele
Los Angeles

His was the best kept secret in Hollywood:

"I'm the only person in the world who knows the story of the ruby slippers — 'I Discovered the Ruby Slippers By Kent Warner.' And Kent Warner bursts into laughter at his own dramatics."

Los Angeles Times

"TAP THREE TIMES"

In Hollywood everything starts with a rumor, like the one I heard in September of 1986 about Ted Turner, owner of the Atlanta Braves, the cable television conglomerate, the MGM film library, and at least one 12-meter yacht. Turner, the story went, had personally searched the shelves of the MGM script vault for an original screenplay from *Gone With The Wind* to take home to Atlanta and proudly display on his living room coffee table. It was wild enough to be true.

A hot September day had me sweating, and not just because of the heat. I was working for a low-budget syndicated television show called *Hollywood Closeup,* and after four years the show was on the fence, struggling for profit. The financiers of the operation decided they wanted to change the show's look and attitude.

The producer, Sherry Weinman, asked me to fill three weekly minutes of air time with sassy, fun roundups of inside industry information, from the perspective of a beat reporter working the streets and green rooms of Hollywood — not quite gossip, but stories with a hint of Hedda Hopper. "Something that bites without breaking the skin," Sherry told me.

I took on producing this segment with misgivings. I knew little about Hollywood, its machinations or its history.

I had my nose in a newspaper and a bagel in my mouth when a slender brunette with gorgeous eyes walked into my office. Her name was Lisa Shaffer, and our relationship was purely professional. She was the show's associate producer and she passed me the rumor on Ted Turner.

The media mogul had been making business headlines for months with his attempt to buy the CBS television network. When that effort failed, he surprised everyone by buying all of Metro-Goldwyn-Mayer in Culver City for a billion dollars. Then, he quickly broke the gigantic old studio into pieces, selling off this building and that name and keeping only the MGM library of films for himself.

Turner held a big news conference, claiming that the studio would continue producing movies, but he really wanted the huge catalogue of films to play on his cable SuperStation. The MGM library contained more than 3,000 titles.

The physical plant of the studio — the building, the land, the film processing laboratory — was sold to the up-and-coming Lorimar-Telepictures, which went on to produce a series of network television successes, including *Dallas*. The MGM name and Leo the Lion logo were sold back to another mogul, Kirk Kerkorian, along with paper assets including all the script properties that had never been produced.

When Turner bought the library of films, he also bought the scripts that went with the movies. Thus the MGM script library was split in half.

I found all this out by calling the script library to check the Turner rumor. Marion Kidd, the librarian there, explained what was really happening. They were in the process, she said, of dividing the script library, and everything was being packed into cardboard boxes for shipment off the lot.

"It's sad right now," she told me, "because the studio is being dismantled. The scripts are being packed up. A lot of them will be lost, or thrown out. We're trying to keep everything together. Many of them are falling apart."

She said there were more than 9,000 properties, maybe a quarter of a million scripts. Without question, the MGM script collection was one of the world's largest archives of Hollywood history and now the collection would not remain intact. That became the headline story of my first *Hollywood Closeup* segment.

* * *

Getting permission to visit the dying script vault would have to come from Roger Mayer. He was the president of the studio and made such decisions.

I thought I'd be talking to his secretary, then writing a letter, and then waiting two weeks for an answer. In two weeks, I figured, I'd either be fired or working on a different segment. But I called anyway. The woman who answered the phone heard me out, then she asked me to hold a minute. Seconds later, Roger Mayer was on the phone, saying yes to my request!

* * *

The Irving Thalberg Building was the brain trust of MGM where everything began and ended. For the good part of half a century, ideas emanated from the minds of men on the second floor of the Thalberg Building and drifted like little clouds through the windows and over the studio wall into a world where busy people manufactured dreams for a living. When the dream-makers had finished their work, a film and its scripts came back to the Thalberg Building, where they were stored in the basement.

I arrived at the Thalberg Building on a bright Friday morning with a camera crew. The two men unloaded their gear while I surveyed the area. Things looked business-as-usual, with people coming and going through the studio gate, but the huge sign that loomed over Stage 6 told the real story: *Running Scared.*

We went by elevator to the basement of the Thalberg Building where the doors opened into an orange-colored world. We went to the caged, east end of the long, concrete cavern that had the distinguished but harsh look and musty smell of a manuscript room in a major library. There I met the librarian, Marion Kidd.

The room was packed with wood and metal shelves that were filled with brown accordion file folders, which in turn were filled with blue-covered scripts. The aisles were lit only by single bulbs that hung from the low ceiling.

The scripts were filed only by the chronological date they had first appeared in the vault. The script for *Ben Hur,* MGM's first film, was stacked high on the oldest shelf, in a dark corner of the big room and scripts for *2010* were at the other end. In between sat countless treasures.

Two of my literary heroes had spent time at MGM during the 1930s: William Faulkner and F. Scott Fitzgerald. I wanted to see any of their scripts that remained. Faulkner had first come to Hollywood in 1932, when Louis B. Mayer signed the not yet Nobel Prize winner to a lucrative contract, in the belief that writers of good books would write good movies. It was an experiment that didn't work. Faulkner was given no assignments, but instead was left to write what he wanted. He grew bored on the job, writing nothing more than a series of stories that amounted to deep and flavorful character sketches. One was called *Manservant.* I found it still in the vault.

Marion Kidd said that *Manservant* belonged to Kirk Kerkorian because it had not been produced. I leafed through the yellow onion-skin paper, filled with a star-struck excitement people usually reserve for the living. "This is priceless," I said. Marion nodded and put the script back on the shelf.

On the floor of another aisle was an overloaded cardboard packing box on which the single word "woman" had been marked crudely in black. It contained a screenplay from *The Women,* a 1939 movie starring Joan Crawford and Norma Shearer. I knew that F. Scott Fitzgerald had worked on the film.

Fitzgerald arrived in Hollywood in July, 1937, with a fat MGM contract and the belief that the movies would save his career. Mayer paid him $1,000 a week, but Fitzgerald's work only fizzled, which frustrated the writer. Fitzgerald's biggest complaint was how much scripts changed.

It wasn't long before Fitzgerald was relegated to priming and polishing other people's scripts; he became a glorified Hollywood copy editor. Because of his debts, he accepted the role, and later that year was assigned to rescue *The Women*. He described Clare Booth Luce's play as a "rather god-awful hodgepodge of bitter wit and half-digested information which titillated New York audiences for over a year." He called his work on the film "cleaning it up for Norma Shearer."

In spite of my deference to the more literary names, I decided to focus my television story on the dismantling of the vault on *The Wizard of Oz*. The image of putting little Dorothy and all her fantastic friends into a cardboard box seemed universally accessible to a television audience.

I asked my guide if I could see the older scripts from *The Wizard of Oz*. There was a box full of them on the floor. From it she pulled Noel Langley's screen adaptation of L. Frank Baum's *fin de siècle* fairy tale, dated May 14, 1938. It was one of the credited screenwriter's early working drafts, full of added pages, scratch-outs and revisions. I perused its yellowed pages which had suffered badly from acid damage, the cancer of paper. On those pages I found History.

Page 26. Scene No. 113. Right where Glinda the Good Witch of the North waves her wand and the shoes belonging to the recently squished Wicked Witch of the East magically appear on the feet of an unexpecting Dorothy. The directorial cue read: *CLOSE UP SILVER SHOES*.

In Baum's book, one of the Munchkins says to Dorothy, "The Witch of the East was proud of those silver shoes... and there is some charm connected with them; but what it is we never knew."

We never knew either, because the *silver* shoes were never seen on the silver screen. *The Wizard of Oz* was big in every Hollywood sense of the word. Louis B. Mayer spent more than three million Depression dollars to produce a movie using Kodak's expensive three-strip Technicolor film. He wasn't going to settle for black-and-white shoes.

Sometime between May 14 and June 4 of 1938 — the last recorded revision date marked on the blue cover of Langley's script — a Hollywood decision was made: the typed word *silver* was rubbed out and *ruby* was written in. By the stroke of a hand, Dorothy Gale's silver shoes became Judy Garland's ruby slippers.

* * *

I had the camera crew photograph the *Oz* script, along with the works by Faulkner and Fitzgerald. It was enough on which to build two television minutes telling the story of the end of the MGM script vault. When I got back to the *Hollywood Closeup* offices, I was filled with energy. I went into Sherry's office, where we viewed the raw tape. She was fascinated by the *Oz* script and asked, "What's the script worth?"

In the context of a television segment, it was a good question. But I didn't have an answer. Since I knew so little about Hollywood, I had no idea that there was a market for such collectibles. If I could get an estimate, I could put that information into the segment.

I called a couple of book stores that advertised in show business trade papers, places that said they bought and sold rare books and manuscripts. "Bring it in," they all said. No one would say over the phone, and I didn't have it in my possession. I started calling libraries, universities, and then the Academy of Motion Picture Arts and Sciences. No answer. I was spending too much time on one question. My last call was to the Smithsonian.

* * *

Three weeks later, Smithsonian curator Carl Scheele called me back. The *Oz* piece had been finished for more than two weeks, but still hadn't aired. Had it already aired, I might have told Scheele that my question was moot. Instead, I asked the value of the script.

Scheele looked miles beyond my question. "We have high regard for such a property," he said. "It has tremendous research value. As you may know, we have the ruby slippers in our collection, but very little ancillary material from *The Wizard of Oz*. Do you own the script?"

"No," I answered. And I hadn't known that the Smithsonian had the ruby slippers.

"Do you know who does own the script?"

"Yes," I told him, "the Turner Entertainment Co."

"We would be very pleased to have a donation from Mr. Turner," Scheele said.

His words startled me. I wrote them down on paper, and stared at them, as we continued our discussion. He was serious. I told him I would convey the message to Roger Mayer, which I did in a flash.

"Yes," Mayer said. "We are very interested in making such a donation. Have the Smithsonian make their request through my office."

Now, not only did I have a good story, but I was in the middle of it. I called Mr. Scheele back to inform him of Mayer's good news, and told the curator I was excited about putting this new information on *Hollywood Closeup*. He was happy to hear the positive response, but asked that I withhold my story until the donation was complete.

The problem was twofold, he explained. When news gets out that the Smithsonian has received a certain item, people come to Washington to see it, and it's hard to explain that the museum doesn't yet have it. Also, since donations take time and often involve anonymous people, any advance word of a gift could foul the deal.

With every donation to the U. S. government museum, a rigmarole of papers have to be signed, including the deed of gift and necessary tax deductions, all of which amount to layers of bureaucracy. Scheele explained that there is also the matter of copyright, especially in the case of a script. When the Smithsonian takes possession of a donation, it becomes government property. Certain precautions were necessary to protect the renewable copyright of the *Oz* script for Turner.

Given the complexity of a donation, information had to be shared in stages. Scheele requested that "public notice of such a gift be withheld until the gift is completed and the script is in our custody, and, perhaps, on public exhibition."

I staggered into Sherry's office. "Remember when you asked how much that *Wizard of Oz* script was worth? The Smithsonian wants it," I said, "and Turner's going to donate it."

"What a great story," she said. "We can get it on this week." "No we can't," I told her. "I promised we'd keep it quiet until the donation is complete." It was a promise I'd have a hard time keeping.

* * *

In one respect, Carl Scheele's reaction to the *Oz* script was a measure of the popularity of the ruby slippers. They had been on display at the Smithsonian for only seven years, yet the crush of humanity passing in front of the exhibit had left the carpet badly worn. In that period the rug had been replaced twice and patched many times. Millions of people, maybe five million a year, had visited the ruby slippers, Scheele said.

The slippers are located on the second floor of the National Museum of American History, along the western wall. They are the centerpiece of a long, glass-enclosed exhibit on American entertainment. The wall is papered with turn-of-the-century sheet music and vaudeville posters reminiscent of Diamond Jim Brady's heyday on Broadway, Chatauqua notices heralding the arrival of small-town road shows, lobby cards from early movie houses, and program covers and photographs including a life-size blowup of the legendary Louis Armstrong — Satchmo.

Behind the glass are national treasures: a lion's harness from *The Greatest Show On Earth,* John L. Sullivan's championship belt, Edgar Bergen's puppet pal, Charlie McCarthy, sitting atop Irving Berlin's upright piano, Archie Bunker's living room chair, and Fonzie's leather motorcycle jacket. Every item conjures up a familiar image in the minds of visitors. But no image is stronger than that of the ruby slippers.

Double takes are common. People see the slippers and are inexplicably drawn toward them. They call over family members, shout out the names of friends, take flash photographs, whisper, point, and talk to themselves about the ruby slippers. In this kingdom of inanimate objects, a pair of red-sequined shoes commands all the subjects.

The most telling sight is in the eyes of children. A little girl, no more than four years old, walks up to the display case and puts her tiny hand to the glass in front of the slippers. "Magic," is all she says. Magic indeed, if you believe. First you have to believe that they are Judy Garland's shoes.

The display card says that they are "the ruby slippers worn by Judy Garland (Frances Gumm) in the 1939 MGM film *The Wizard of Oz*." But Carl Scheele told me better. "We backed away from the original claim that Judy Garland wore the shoes, but we do claim they are from the production and she starred in it."

Scheele's admission caught me by surprise. Were these not the *real* ruby slippers? They were real enough, he said, but other pairs of ruby slippers were made for the movie, including pairs reputedly made for stand-ins. The Smithsonian had no way of knowing if its pair was actually worn by Judy Garland. To collectors of Hollywood memorabilia, I guessed this distinction mattered. Scheele also wanted to know the answer. "If you find out," he said, "let me know."

* * *

Television research is shallow. One phone call is usually enough and two or three classified the story as "in-depth." Usually, there isn't time to dig much deeper, as everything is always "going to air." But because of my deal with Scheele, I had time to ask another question: How many pairs of slippers? To research that, I called the old wardrobe department at MGM.

A voice answered and sounded friendly. I explained myself, asked my question, and was met with silence. Then the voice laughed.

"Oh God, you're not going to get into that?"

"Into what?" I said.

"I don't even know—there's more than one pair though."

That was sinking in. "How many?" I bluntly asked.

"That's a good question. I don't know how many. One pair was sold at the MGM auction in the 1970s, and one pair is at the Smithsonian—I think they were donated by Liza Minnelli. Sammy Davis, Jr. may have a pair. I heard that, and another pair disappeared before the auction. They were taken by somebody close to the auction, you know what I mean?"

"You mean a pair was stolen?"

"I didn't say that. I don't really know what happened."

"Then what are you telling me?" I asked.

"There's a pair that belongs to a lady in the South, but those were for Judy's stand-in, and then another pair were stolen in San Francisco... "

"So, that's one, two, three," I counted. "That's six pairs."

"Maybe," said the voice.

"Maybe?"

"Maybe there's more. I'm not the right person to ask."

"Who is?"

"I don't know if anyone is. Well, one person knew."

"Who's that?"

"Kent Warner. He had a pair of the slippers. He worked for the auction. He had a pair of ruby slippers in his living room. There was an article about him in the paper."

"Kent Warner," I repeated, spelling out his name.

"Yes."

"Where can I find him?" I asked.

"You can't," the voice said. "He's dead."

"Dead?" I repeated.

"Mm-hmm... "

"Did he have any family?"

"Good luck. His mother, maybe." The voice told me her name.

"Any friends?"

"Only one I know. Joe. He had the witch's hat."

"Huh?"

"Margaret Hamilton's witch hat, from the movie."

"Oh—"

"Kent gave it to Joe. Maybe Joe could help you."

"Great."

"—but listen, I can't talk about this now, I've got people calling me and producers are on my back for costumes and I don't have any help today."

"I understand," I said.

"Maybe you could come down here and we could talk about it some other time?"

"Sure," I said, thinking about lunch.

"Some morning," the voice suggested, "before 8:30. I can talk then."

* * *

"WELCOME TO THE LAND OF OZ"

In the year of my birth, CBS-TV negotiated with Metro-Goldwyn-Mayer for rights to broadcast *The Wizard of Oz* as a once-a-year television special. The arrangement, originally designed as a two- or three-year deal, resulted in one of the more remarkable successes of network television. *Oz* quickly became a perennial favorite for children and adults alike.

The CBS debut of *Oz* came on November 3, 1956. Thirty years later, I figured I had seen the movie more than a dozen times and never once had it occured to me that there might be more than one pair of ruby slippers. What was common knowledge among Hollywood costumers and people inside the film business — that doubles and triples of every important costume must exist on every set in case of damage or wear — was news to me.

So imagine the surprise of Roberta Jefferies Bauman, of Memphis, Tennessee, when she sat down to coffee on the morning of May 18, 1970, and read in her newspaper that "the ruby red slippers... fetched $15,000" at an historic MGM auction in Los Angeles. Roberta had in her closet a pair of the ruby slippers she won in a contest in 1940!

The article said the shoes had been purchased by Richard Wonder, "who identified himself as a representative of a 'Southern California millionaire.'"

"It was real exciting," Roberta drawled. "I called the paper right away and said 'I have a pair of the ruby red slippers' and that's when all the commotion started!"

Very quickly, her story tickled the news wires across the country. Roberta Jeffries had been a junior at Humes High School in Memphis when MGM released *The Wizard of Oz* in 1939. "I was a member of the *Photoplay* Club," she said. "It was organized by our teacher, Miss Josephine Allensworth, who was interested in films. She and Miss Lucille Patton organized the group.

"Back in those days people were concerned about the quality of films, and Miss Allensworth was active with the Better Films Council. If they didn't think a picture was fit to come in to town, they did something about it. We had some strict judges back in those days.

"So Miss Josephine and Miss Lucille organized this group and it met after school. As part of the *Photoplay* Club activities, we were given passes to the movies and we'd go to the movies in pairs. We would take notes, and afterwards we would come back to the club and report on the movies.

"We had to rate the films like prize-winning books. And there were a lot of good films that year.

"I can't recall if *The Wizard of Oz* was the favorite of the bunch. It was impressive, and some people went overboard about it — to each his own. *Oz* was just a fantastic fairy tale, but there were a lot of other films.

"I saw *Pygmalion, Oz, Mr. Smith Goes to Washington; Goodbye Mr. Chips* was very popular too, and *Gone With the Wind,* of course.

"Toward the end of the year, Miss Josephine had us vote on all the pictures. Through her affiliation with the Better Films Council, she was a member of the National Four-Star Club, which had something to do with picking the year's ten best movies. She had every one of us send in our votes on a penny postcard. My gosh, I can't even remember how I voted.

"Later, I guess it was February of 1940, Miss Josephine told me and Will Bowden that we both had won second place in the contest. I couldn't believe it."

Will Bowden couldn't believe it either. "It was remarkable that the two of us won," he said from his home in Montgomery, Alabama.

On Saturday, February 24, one of the Memphis newspapers announced that two local students were second-prize winners in the National Four-Star Club's contest for selection of the ten best pictures of 1939. They would be awarded their prizes the following Tuesday, February 27, at 10:30 in the morning.

"We went to school that day," Roberta remembered, "and then we were given permission to get out of school. Miss Josephine took us over to midtown, and we went to this exclusive club, the 19th Century Club. It was fancy.

"We had a little program, a couple of typical reviews and a skit or two, and then the club president introduced us, Will and me, and Miss Josephine presented us with our prizes. He received the gavel from *Mr. Smith Goes to Washington,* the one used by Harry Carey, and I received Judy Garland's ruby red shoes.

"I didn't get anything with the shoes. Miss Josephine said they had come from a Hollywood exhibit in New York City. They were handed to me in a pasteboard shoe box.

"I took them home and even tried them on to show them to my mom and daddy, and of course, then, I just put them up in the wardrobe. They were so delicate I did not want to destroy them. I put them up there for protection. Whenever somebody came over and asked about the shoes, I'd show them.

"Of course, hardly anybody cared much about the shoes after that. The War was on and everybody had to concentrate on that. I was married on May 8, 1944. VE Day. My husband went over to England on June 6, same year, and we were separated until September, 1945. I stayed at my mother's until then, and the ruby red slippers were always in my possession.

"There wasn't any activity from then on until 1959, when my first son started school, then I showed the shoes to his class. All the kids loved them, so for my other kids, I did the same thing. Sometimes, I'd put them on display at the library around the time that the movie was on television.

"The last time they were on display was in 1968, when Martin Luther King was assassinated in this town. They were on display at the Memphis Public Library. I went and got them that day and took them home and didn't put them on display again.

"When 1970 came, I didn't expect what happened. I hadn't heard anything about that auction until it came out in the morning paper that day. The first thing I did was call Miss Josephine and said, 'Remember, you gave us those properties?' She said, 'I challenge you to call the paper and ask about it,' and that's where the controversy started.

"I felt in my heart that they had to be an original pair, so I called up there at the paper and I said, 'I too have a pair of those ruby red slippers.' They told me to come up there with the shoes. I sat at the desk and they kept handling them.

"After they printed another story, I sat down and wrote a letter to MGM in Culver City.

'I would like to hear from MGM regarding the pair of Judy Garland shoes I received in 1940. Since Mr. Wonder paid such a price for the pair he got at the auction, I wanted to establish the fact if he had the original or do I have the original?

'I have cherished these shoes for all these years and each time this film has been rerun on television I have put this pair on display at the Memphis Public Library and many children have seen them. So for the benefit of my children and also Mr. Wonder's client, I felt I had a right to question their value. To seek out an honest answer would clarify the fact if I have been misled for these 30 years.'

"I sent the letter and it came back marked 're-fused.' They didn't even open it. I think it was kind of rude. I was just asking a common sense question. I wanted to be clear. I didn't want to go around falsifying anything."

By the time the letter came back, Roberta Bauman's surprise had turned into the realization that the Land of Oz was a very different place from the Land of Hollywood.

* * *

For all of Roberta Bauman's surprise, imagine the shock felt by the "Southern California millionaire" when the *Memphis Press-Scimitar* reported the existence of another pair of ruby shoes. Assuming the property unique, he had sent his representative, Mr. Wonder of Newport Beach, to the auction with the authority to spend up to $22,000 for the slippers. $15,000 must have seemed a steal.

But another pair? Was this anonymous buyer upset? Roberta Bauman hadn't paid anything for her pair of slippers; he had paid dearly. The slippers were the most expensive costume sold at the auction. To add insult to injury, Debbie Reynolds had claimed that the auction shoes weren't even Judy Garland's, they were "too big." People said they were stand-in shoes. The millionaire had a right to be peeved.

How many pairs were there, he must have wondered? What was one pair really worth? If they weren't unique, what were they? Were they fakes? Were they stand-in shoes? Who knew? But there definitely were other pairs, which had to make the "Southern California millionaire" feel less than great.

The name of the buyer was protected from the press by his agent, Mr. Wonder, but Bauman said she had heard the man was so angry, "he wished he'd never seen the bloody red shoes." She was sorry about that, if it was her doing, but she could do no more than tell the truth.

It probably wasn't Roberta Bauman who ticked the man off; he was probably angry at the auctioneers, then at himself, for being so naïve. He was a perfect example of Hollywood's magical hold over the mass of people, willing to believe what ears hear and eyes see.

Here were *the* ruby slippers, in real life, as they had been on the screen. One mysterious pair, revered, under a spotlight in the center of a room.

The magic of the movie remains firmly in the minds of the believers, but so much reverence poured into a pair of sequined shoes seemed somewhat ludicrous when the lights were turned off and the costumers began talking their lingo of "doubles" and "triples." Certainly there would be more than one pair of ruby slippers. How could Mr. Wonder's man have missed that? Easy. Almost everyone else did.

Once corrected, the millionaire could only guess with others how many pairs of ruby slippers really existed. It was anybody's guess, and nobody, it seemed, really knew.

"We have records in which certain information is held in confidence," Carl Scheele told me. I asked him the name of the person who donated the ruby slippers to the Smithsonian. But the slippers on public display at the museum, he said, "were acquired from MGM in 1970 by the donor for $15,000. He's the only link between us and MGM. He held them for a decade."

I supposed that the donor had taken a big tax deduction, which the government allows on important contributions to the nation's archives. The Smithsonian is not generally in the practice of disputing estimations of value for artifacts they deem "priceless" by the very request to place it in the museum; nor do they make such figures available to the public.

People donate for different reasons, Scheele explained. "Money is a great motivator. Frankly, at certain times people need to make a gift in terms of their income taxes. Sometimes people who are otherwise well off become worried when they sit on a well-known property. They don't want to get knocked off or burgled. Sometimes it's a combination of all these things."

Scheele had seen his share of donations. He said museum acquisitions in his department averaged one transaction a day. My contact with Mr. Scheele was during the final months of his career. In November, 1987, he retired, after nearly 30 years with the museum.

To the National Museum of American History, Scheele was something of a Professor Marvel. He assumed the same physical stature as the traveling prognosticator played by Frank Morgan in *The Wizard of Oz*. Scheele considered the ruby slippers among his favorite acquisitions from Hollywood, along with the "Piccolino" dress worn by Ginger Rogers in *Top Hat*.

His favorite acquisition, Scheele said, was "a post office, built in 1860," which came to the Institution from Headsville, West Virginia. The post office, which was also a general store, is now a "living museum" where visitors to the Smithsonian may deposit mail and get a special postmark, provided by the Postal Service.

Also high on Scheele's list of acquisitions was a Yankee Stadium ticket booth from 1923, the year the stadium opened. ("George Steinbrenner gave us that at the end of the 1974 baseball season.") Scheele also found a 100-year-old schoolroom in his native Cleveland, which the city Board of Education had planned to demolish but instead donated. Then there was "a whole bandstand from Jacksonville, Illinois, which was beautifully preserved. We could scrape it down and see how many times it had been painted," Scheele beamed. These larger items were favorites, he said, because they "hold a lot of history."

Hollywood was one of his late-blossoming interests. "Some of the best creative talents of the century worked for Hollywood," he said, but he lamented the difficulty of obtaining gifts. On one occasion, a reporter for the *Washington Post* wrote a story about the museum's interest in collecting Hollywood memorabilia; in it, the reporter published "a wish list" of items Scheele wanted to acquire.

"Frank Sinatra had the best reaction," Scheele remembered. "On the wish list, I included Sinatra's bow ties." The list was reprinted in the *Los Angeles Times,* where Scheele presumed Sinatra saw it. Several weeks later, he said, "We received a box with two bow ties, but no cover letter. It had the return address, to which we sent a deed of gift, which came back with Frank's signature. No demands, no publicity. It made us feel real good. Just a nice, straightforward gift."

Sadly, Scheele said, other Hollywood memorabilia has not been so easy to get: "We learned some things were beyond reach. Fred Astaire, for example, didn't have anything. Very few, if any, of Ginger Rogers' gowns were preserved, because by the end of her shooting, most were worn out. There's also a problem in management's mind about people who are still around. A donation could be interpreted as advertising. Sometimes it does appear that we're telling the world something is important because we've collected it."

But the most difficult problem with Hollywood has been finding people who care about preservation. "Corporations characteristically have no recognition of their own history," Scheele said. But they were not solely to blame. "Widows and children have thrown out collections. It's remarkable that any of it survived."

At the time Scheele and I spoke, I had no idea that soon I would fall into a peculiar underworld, where a few highly-charged and dedicated individuals operated with stealth and secrecy to preserve the material remnants of Hollywood's history. Soon I would find myself scratching and clawing for truth at this underworld's dark center. This was a world, I learned, that held as its prize, the *pièce de résistance,* the ruby slippers.

* * *

A COWARDLY LION

The voice that had told me on the phone about Kent Warner became a face when I visited the ghosts of Hollywood past at MGM's Wardrobe Department in Culver City. His one demand was anonymity and so, in the spirit of the studio, I'll call him "Leo." The hour we met was ungodly, but Leo greeted me with a cup of coffee and a touch of nerves. The phone rang and work called.

"Feel free to look around while I take care of some business. I won't be more than fifteen minutes," Leo said.

I had never seen such a place. The Wardrobe Department filled a two-story building; below were offices, and above were clothes. There were clothes on racks built on racks, reaching to the ceiling. Army clothes, suits of fine English cloth, pressed white shirts, tuxedos, dresses, coats of leather, fur, and denim, blue jeans, chaps, cowboy shirts, hats, helmets, belts, buckles, boots, wing tips, high heels, flats, clogs, and a ton of makeshift jewelry and accessories. In the office area were walls of books and file cabinets filled with sketches. In the short time I was left alone, I canvassed everything, then Leo came back.

"Quite a collection," I said.

"Not really, There's not much left. We used to have much more, so much more, and that was *after* the auction. I can't imagine how much was here before."

We talked briefly about the slippers and then about Kent Warner.

"I knew Kent for twelve years, since 1972. He did the set-up for the auction. He sorted through everything and was responsible for all the photos in the catalog."

I asked for a physical description of this man.

"He was five-ten, naturally curly hair, sandy blond, a Jewish nose, and sometimes a moustache — a good-looking man. He always took care of himself. Very fastidious and career-oriented. A borderline workaholic and very detail-oriented."

Leo knew some of the story of the ruby slippers.

"Let's think like Kent Warner," Leo said. These were words I'd remember. "He was hired in 1970 to work on the auction."

"Who hired him?" I asked.

"I don't know, I have no idea. The auctioneers?"

Then Leo continued: "He was in Lot 2, now condos, sorting through 30, 40 years of stored wardrobes, finding items for the auction. A dirty, filthy job, inches of dust. There was a lot of the *The Great Zeigfeld* stuff, plus *Oz* and everything else. It was a giant sound stage, used as a closet, unopened for 20 years. He searched, day by day, for weeks, looking into every locker, every chest, every bin.

"In one bin he found three or four inches of dust. Beneath the dust, a bundle, wrapped in muslin. He picked it up and unraveled the cloth and out they fell. Three pairs of ruby slippers — a size 6, one unmarked, and one with 'Judy Garland 5B' stitched in. The shoes were old, sequins faded, roughed up, but Kent knew exactly what he'd found. He had gone into the job knowing he might find the ruby slippers and in many ways he pursued them."

"Three pairs... " I mumbled.

"That's what he said. He could have found more. I heard there were six. Suppose he *kept* three pairs and didn't tell anyone, you know what I mean?"

I asked some more about Kent — where he worked, his friends.

"For many years, he worked at Universal, through most of the 1970s. He had an office there for a while. Then he went to Stephen J. Cannell, where he became head of the Wardrobe Department. He had a credit on *The A-Team,* which he was very proud of. I think that was his last."

Leo saddened when we talked about Kent's death.

"He denied having AIDS. And his mother denied it. She was his best friend, but her behavior was always obsessive. She loved her son. Kent was one of the early AIDS victims. He was a very private person. He didn't tell anyone. Toward the end, when I was calling to see what I could do, his mother said, 'Nothing, he's fine.'

"Kent always wanted the slippers to go into a museum, but after his death, his mother sold all his personal effects, possibly to pay doctor bills. Many things were purchased by a close friend of his, Paul Tiberio. Paul died last month. It's such a tragedy. Kent's mother could be helping other mothers." Then Leo's voice gave way to a trail of hidden tears, and he whispered: "Isn't truth stranger than fiction?"

* * *

THE RAGS OF SHADOWS

The MGM auction in May, 1970 was like an 18-day wake for Hollywood. People wailed and cursed the death of the giant studio while picking the flesh off the corpse, clean to the bone. Everyone seemed to agree it was the symbolic end of the Golden Era of the Silver Screen.

The Times of London called it the "Tatters of an Empire" and wrote:

> "Auctions are always melancholy: it is the speed and inevitability with which the evidences of a lifetime can be dispersed. Perhaps the reason why this sale is more melancholy than most is that in a way it is all our lives, the dreams which we have for so many years bought from a Hollywood which can never be the same... Once they sold shadows; and now they are selling the rags of shadows."

MGM was felled by the mightiest sword of all: a banker's pen. The evidence of Louis B. Mayer's lifetime amounted to the largest movie-making warehouse in the world, but to the big, bottom-liners who ran the studio in 1970, it was nothing but a burden of storage and maintenance. They looked over their back lots and saw a lot of junk. Time to have a yard sale; what they couldn't sell, they would dump.

The auction was conceived by a Los Angeles businessman named David Weisz, who, in professional parlance, specialized in liquidating. Weisz came from a family of auctioneers and was known as the "man with the golden gavel." He could sell anything, "from an entire Northern California town to the ruby slippers that whisked Dorothy home to Kansas."

Late in 1969, Weisz learned that MGM chairman Kirk Kerkorian was selling studio property to finance a Grand Hotel and casino in Las Vegas. He was selling the land west of Overland Avenue to developers, for condominiums. The contents of Studio Lots 2, 3, 4 and 5 had to be cleared out before the buildings were razed. Weisz made a deal with Kerkorian: for about $1.5 million, he'd buy everything, lock, stock and barrel, ship, car and caboose.

To the crafty Kerkorian, the money must have seemed great for all that "junk"; Weisz, on the other hand, had no idea what he bought. There was furniture, he knew, mostly antiques, and Weisz had a good eye for such things. By selling the furniture, Weisz expected to make his money back. But in no way could Weisz comprehend the immensity, or the eccentricity, of Louis B. Mayer's Movieland collection. "We bought more than just general equipment," Weisz said. "We bought a myth."

The "myth" included an unbelievable assortment of treasures, from cannon carriages, horse buggies and monstrous Conestogas from the Old West, to Roman chariots, manufactured for *Ben Hur* in 1926. There were fine cut glass chandeliers from Vienna, marble statues, magic boxes, jeweled knives, model ships and trains, dolls, suits of armor, grandfather clocks and chairs, row after row, aisle after aisle, chairs in every style of every age dating back to the dawn of man.

There were double-decker busses, a space capsule, royal coaches and candelabrums; a working locomotive from the 19th century and countless railroad cars, a submarine, fishing boats, and a full-sized sailing ship from *Mutiny on the Bounty*. There were bicycles, and tanks, half-tracks and jeeps, some of them marked with the German Iron Cross, or Nazi swastika. The big paddle wheeler from *Showboat* was floating in a man-made lake. There were airplanes of World War II vintage, tugboats, pleasure craft, and dozens of automobiles. There were diving bells, anchors, armoires and easy chairs, dressers, bureaus, old oak desks, divans, ottomans, and tables.

The inventory that Kerkorian sold represented a lifetime of collecting for Mayer. He had dressed his films in props that were absolutely authentic.

Kerkorian might have taken all of Mayer's furnishings to his new hotel in the desert and adorned the gaudy modern palace with Hollywood treasures, but no such thought occurred to the great financier. No one had yet started the selling of movie memories—and it wasn't a concept about which Kerkorian cared.

His ignorance of Hollywood's historic impact was shared, not just by his contemporaries at other studios, but by the very men who made Hollywood, including Mayer. None of the founders had the sentimental wherewithal to understand the value of their own past. In certain respects, these were romantic men. But a good romance to them was a box-office smash. Who would have thought that movie memorabilia would someday be worth good money to fans?

It was a concept that even the shrewd David Weisz didn't fully comprehend, but one that a young costumer on the MGM lot in the Spring of 1970 understood completely.

David Weisz knew exactly what he would do with the cars, props, trains and furniture, but the 350,000 costumes that came with the package were a mystery. For advice, Weisz called upon his son-in-law, Richard Carroll, a prominent merchandiser and retail clothier in Beverly Hills.

Richard Carroll, owner of the fashionable Carroll and Co. on Rodeo Drive, told me what he remembered:

"David called me, probably before he bought the MGM properties, and asked me to look at the costumes. Twenty-two minutes, I figured, that's how much time I would give him. I had no idea.

"We went down to the lot, to where the costumes were. There were seven warehouses—sound stages!—full of props and costumes. There must have been 500 Munchkin costumes, all beautifully put together, fabulous costumes, but what do you do with them? There were prison costumes, military costumes, Nazi costumes, damn Nazi costumes right there. I wouldn't sell them. I burned them. Sell a Nazi costume, are you kidding?

"I told David I didn't know what we could do with the costumes, to let me think about it. The costumes must have come as part of the deal. They weren't thrown in, like you might think. Look at the studio at the time. James Aubrey, a friend of mine, was president of the studio. He had to look at these warehouses and ask what the studio was doing in the junk business. All this junk they were maintaining for what? He wasn't very sentimental about it, nor should he have been. These things were a tremendous burden to the studio at the time. I can't tell you about the deal. I never asked, I never knew, it was none of my business, but David made some kind of deal, you can bet, for the costumes. A dollar a costume, maybe, or less. But they were sold, not for what they were, but as units. 350,000 units, so many dollars. David had to do something with them.

"In January or February of 1970, I guess, I was in Europe when David called me and we talked about the costumes. I told him, look, the only way to go is to have a retail sale. I was looking at the fashion of the day. Come on, old ladies weren't going to buy this stuff. I was going to have a retail sale for the kids, a big hippie sale. It wasn't until we started finding out what kind of costumes were there that we decided to auction anything.

"My wife, Judy, deserves a lot of the credit. We began finding wonderful costumes, so I told David, let me catalog one thousand costumes, and we'll have an auction. I convinced him. But to have an auction, I said, we needed a set, and we needed the carpenters and the technicians. We wanted to put on a show. And that's what we did.

"Of course, David got us the set and everything we wanted. He would have done anything for Judy, his daughter, and she was so excited. The auction became something special. It wasn't a problem for David to get us what we wanted. He simply called up James Aubrey, who was happy to help out. I don't know if he even charged us for the use of the set.

"I said we'd give him a thousand costumes. We found 5,000. Do you have any idea how many cowboy outfits there were? People thought we were insane, and we were.

"We talked about having ten different auctions. We had five. We had a Cowboy auction, and an Indian auction. But the best attended was the first, when we sold the ruby slippers.

"Believe me, we had some amazing pieces of wardrobe, but nothing compared to the ruby slippers. I think they were the most important thing in the auction. If I were Macy's or Tiffany's, I would have bought them for any amount of money in the world."

"We put the slippers in a box, center stage," Carroll said, "with no identification. People didn't need to be told what they were. It was so dramatic, a hush in the air… a magical pair of slippers. People just wanted to be near them."

According to Aljean Harmetz's book *The Making of Ihe Wizard of Oz,* Judy Garland's ruby slippers were found, "wrapped in a Turkish towel in a bin in the basement of MGM's wardrobe department sometime during February or March 1970." She didn't say who found them.

She quoted Richard Carroll, who described the occasion of the find as "very undramatic." He said, "A guy came up to me and said, 'Here are some shoes Judy Garland wore in *The Wizard of Oz*.'"

"A guy?" I asked. "Kent Warner," Carroll said. "He was a Hollywood costumer. Kent Warner found the ruby slippers."

* * *

THE NIGHT OF THE AUCTION

"**K**ent Warner was the creative genius behind the way we displayed the costumes," said Judy Weisz Carroll. She and Warner worked hand-in-hand preparing the Star Wardrobe for the auction. Judy had little working knowledge of costuming, but a lot of enthusiasm. Kent Warner became her wardrobe guru.

"He was so intimately involved with the studio and the wardrobe department," she told me. "He seemed to know what everything was. He could see what the costumes meant to people, and he was very creative."

With virtual carte blanche, Kent created the showcase of costumes to be auctioned. He found ways to "fly" them in the huge sound stage, so that the gowns rustled with life, as if brushed by an imaginary wind. He did not merely place costumes on hangers; he orchestrated their position on mannequins, in concert with other pieces from the same period. In one section, he created an ensemble of costumes from the many 18th century period films MGM had produced, including the magnificent beaded gown worn by Norma Shearer in *Marie Antoinette*. He gave and gave of himself, filling the inanimate gowns with his enthusiasm; and from the costumes he drew energy.

Nowhere was this energy more evident than in Kent's discovery of the ruby slippers. "Until Kent found the slippers, nobody was very excited about the auction," Judy said.

Jack Haley, Jr. recalled that the shoes were the premiere attraction on MGM's Stage 27 that night, and nobody missed the irony of *The Wizard of Oz* having been produced on that very stage. "The stage was dressed with many costumes," Haley remembered, "and the centerpiece was a pedestal, with a glass bell jar covering the ruby slippers. It wasn't terribly fancy, but very dramatic."

Stars came out for the event, including a voracious Debbie Reynolds, who purchased everything she could afford, and then some. "Debbie was quite frustrated by the time the ruby slippers were auctioned," Haley said. "She ran out of money."

Long before sunset, the public began to fill the rows of red chairs that filled the sound stage; row after row, chair after chair, a sea of red chairs in a hanger-sized room full of clothes. By the time the feature sale began, all the chairs were filled.

"I'll never forget that Sunday," Richard Carroll told me. "The first thing to be sold was Garbo's velvet hat from *Anna Karenina* and David personally took the gavel. He'd retired from auctioning a long time ago. He was the best, the world's greatest auctioneer. He made a lot of money as an auctioneer. Someone like David wasn't going to take that gavel and get embarrassed.

"Judy and I were sitting together and she was nervous. Her hands were shaking. David showed the hat, then said, 'Do I hear a bid?' Then there was this silence. This hadn't been done before. I'm not sure if people knew what to bid.

"Now David wasn't stupid. He would always have a shill in the audience, someone to say, ten, 20 dollars, whatever. I'm not saying that's what happened, but there was this tremendous silence, then somebody made a small bid. Then another, and another, until the hat sold for $300. Then, everything went crazy."

After the Garbo hat, a parade of costumes were sold. Elizabeth Taylor's wedding gown from *Father of the Bride* brought $650; Spencer Tracy's morning coat from the same picture sold for $125. Another Garbo gown, a green velvet dress worn in *Conquest*, went for $550. Clark Gable's "lucky trench coat," which he wore in several pictures, brought $1,250, while Myrna Loy's satin robe from *After the Thin Man* claimed $112.50. They sold Esther Williams' swimsuits, Johnny Weissmuller's *Tarzan* loincloth and Gina Lollobrigida's black lace panties (for $50).

Debbie Reynolds bought her own dress she wore in *How the West Was Won*. Before bidding began on the pink-flowered taffeta gown, Debbie stood up and shouted: "Are you going to give this one away?" $100 was offered, then up and up. "Stop!" Debbie yelled, when the price hit $175, much to the delight of the audience. She finally bought the gown for $200, and the audience applauded.

Debbie bought other items too. She paid $325 for a beaded chiffon gown worn by Grace Kelly in *The Swan*, $50 for a Claire Bloom shawl, another $175 for a hat from *Gigi*, and $325 for a satin gown from *Naughty Marietta,* a Jeanette MacDonald movie. Jeanette MacDonald was a surprise favorite at the auction.

When *Oz* pieces sold, the excitement built. Margaret Hamilton's witch hat sold for $450 (in 1988, the same hat — one of three made for the movie — sold for $33,000 at Sotheby's in New York), and her witch dress went for another $350; Bert Lahr's Cowardly Lion pelt — an actual skin — went for $2,400; Dorothy's blue-and-white checked gingham dress (one of *ten!*) brought $1,000, and Frank Morgan's Wizard suit fetched $650. The prices were considerably out of whack, but couldn't foreshadow the future.

Then came the sale of the ruby slippers, lot W-1048. As a reward for his work, Kent was allowed to carry the pair of slippers from their display case to the podium. For this special occasion, Kent designed a velvet cushion on which he carried the shoes. Kent later told friends it was the highlight of his life.

David Weisz presided, gavel in hand. Richard Wonder, representing the "Southern California millionaire," made the opening bid, $1,000. The price jumped quickly to $11,000, where, wire service reporters said, the bidding momentarily stalled, then rose to $15,000, where it ended. Mr. Wonder had tendered the winning bid.

"They were sold quickly," Carroll said. "I don't recall exactly, something like, 'a thousand, four thousand, five, eight, eleven... ' Then it came down to just a couple of bidders. 'Fifteen thousand dollars,' and that was that. David never expected anything like that amount of money."

"None of us had any idea we'd see that much money for the shoes," said Judy Carroll.

"If somebody had offered David a thousand dollars for the ruby slippers before the auction," Richard Carroll told me, "he would have sold them in a second. He looked at those costumes from a business point of view."

Kent Warner did not. He knew what the ruby slippers were worth. He beamed when the price went through the roof.

The sale of the ruby slippers became national news.

Two days later, pandemonium erupted when Roberta Bauman came forward with her 30-year-old shoe-box containing a bona fide pair of ruby red slippers.

Richard Carroll claimed that there never was any other pair of ruby slippers. "There was never a duplicate of anything," he declared. We had one Clark Gable raincoat, one Garbo dress. We never, never, never heard of another pair of ruby slippers."

Judy Carroll agreed: "I didn't know anything about any other pairs. We couldn't have auctioned those off feeling there was another pair. If another pair had survived, we would have been required to let the public know. What we did, we did with the utmost integrity."

"I never knew about more than one pair of slippers, any place, any time," Richard Carroll maintained. "And if David were alive, he would assure you of the same thing. If David had known about any other pairs, he would have thrown them into the sea."

Of course, more than one pair of ruby slippers had been made for the movie; even Richard Carroll admitted that. But at the time of the auction, he said, the ladies of the MGM wardrobe department had told him only one pair existed. Nobody knew what had happened to the rest. Nobody except Kent Warner, the man who found the slippers.

Kent Warner was thankful that the Bauman discovery didn't arouse any suspicion. He was quiet about Roberta's shoes, hoping to avoid questions. The greatest pinch in Hollywood remained Hollywood's best kept secret. Who was this Kent Warner, this Hollywood costumer? How did he become the "Keeper of the Shoes"? How did he get away with it?

"We called him Kent'ala," Richard Carroll said. "He was a very talented young man — maybe too talented for his own good."

* * *

"FOLLOW THE YELLOW BRICK ROAD"

When the ruby slippers were sent to the Smithsonian Institution in December of 1979, Carl Scheele asked the museum technician Susan Schreiber to handle the donation. Schreiber, he said, would know more of the details surrounding the gift. Now no longer a museum employee, Schreiber was happy to talk to me about the slippers.

"I'm positive there were no marks on the shoes. Judy Garland's name was not on them, no numbers, just the manufacturer's label. INNES shoes. The heel was worn down and the sole was painted red. They looked like red satin shoes with sequins hand-stitched to the shoe, little round ones. I'm pretty sure they're size 5s. I'm a five, and I put my foot in one."

I asked about the donor, and Schreiber told me.

"He said he purchased them at the MGM auction — that is the information that we were given. It's not like he's a famous person or anything. And I think that he approached the Smithsonian."

"For the tax deduction?"

"I'm sure he took a lot larger tax deduction than he paid," Schreiber told me. "He took a much larger deduction."

How, I asked, did she verify their authenticity?

"I sent a lot of correspondence," she said, including letters to the David Weisz Company. "They were not particularly cooperative. You should look at the file on the shoes at the Smithsonian."

* * *

Schreiber began her efforts to verify the authenticity and provenance of the shoes during the winter of 1980. She sent a letter to

David Weisz asking for any information he might have regarding the sale of the slippers at the MGM auction. Weisz responded several months later with a handwritten note on business stationery that read:

> Ms. Schreiber —
> Dick Carroll who physically handled presentation of the wardrobe at the MGM sale is best qualified with details —
> Enclosed is a copy of his recollections — Hope this serves your purpose.
> DW

Attached was a two-page letter Carroll wrote to Weisz on April 24, 1980:

> Dear David:
> Here are my recollections of the circumstances surrounding the "red slippers."
> One day when the crew was preparing the wardrobe ensemble for the first auction of "Star" wardrobe, one of the wardrobe men came to me with a pair of red slippers wrapped in a white towel. They told me that they had discovered the famous red slippers worn by Judy Garland in *The Wizard of Oz* and that these were in fact the actual ones. The wardrobe woman who actually worked in that capacity on the original *The Wizard of Oz* was working for us at the same time and authenticated the slippers. She said that six identical pair had been made for Judy Garland and this was the only pair left. She had no idea where the others were but had a strong feeling that they were used during the actual production and placed in the wardrobe department for future use on other productions. She authen-

ticated the fact that these were in fact the slippers Judy Garland had worn. We cleaned them up and immediately placed them in a safe provided for us, and we kept them until the first showing of the "Star" wardrobe, when we placed them on a wooden pedestal, covered with a velvet top and covered with a glass dome. We never identified the slippers and yet of the 18,000 people who viewed them during that inspection week, not one was unaware of their origin and where they came from.

To further authenticate the slippers, we ran the original movie, *The Wizard of Oz,* where the slippers were very prominent by their presence.

At the time of the sale, a number of people claimed that they too had a pair of the famous red slippers — but none of them ever surfaced and I can't give you the names of those people. There is no question of the authenticity of this particular pair. They were made for Judy Garland and were used by her in the original MGM picture, *The Wizard of Oz.*

I do not think the Smithsonian is interested in anything more than determining authenticity. You can, however, remind them that the slippers are perhaps, in my modest opinion, the single most important object ever photographed and portrayed on the screen. The looks and the hushed remarks of the thousands of people who viewed them at the auction will attest to that.

Sincerely,
Dick

Schreiber, however, was not completely satisfied with this information. Less than a year later, she received a letter from Roberta Bauman, who, upon hearing that the Smithsonian had acquired a pair

of ruby slippers, wanted more information for her own files. Roberta was still trying to determine the authenticity of her shoes. She
hoped Schreiber could provide some of the missing clues. Schreiber
responded, thanking Roberta for her letter, but added little to solve
Roberta's puzzle:

> Dear Mrs. Bauman:
> We received the ruby slippers, which we have on
> exhibit, in December 1979. The donor wishes to re-
> main anonymous, so I regret that I am unable to give
> out his name. We understand that the donor purchased
> the shoes at the MGM auction in 1970.
> When we received the donation I contacted David
> Weisz Co. in Los Angeles, the auction house which
> handled the MGM property auction, to try to obtain
> some background information. I was not very success-
> ful. The questions I asked remained unanswered, and
> they basically gave me the same information which ap-
> pears in Harmetz's book, *The Making of the Wizard of
> Oz...*

Schreiber closed her letter, seemingly resigned in her efforts to
secure the truth. Though intrigued, she let the matter go. The matter, however, did not let go of her.

During the next year, Schreiber received more correspondence
from individuals requesting information about the ruby slippers,
some asking questions for which she had no answers.

No ruby slipper correspondence was more compelling than that
from Julie Collier, assistant vice president of the Collectibles Department at Christie's East, the auction house in New York. Collier asked
for information about the slippers because a pair had been consigned
for public auction. She needed to verify their authenticity.

Collier understandably was concerned about shoe size. The
Smithsonian slippers were size 5C, she had heard that Roberta

Bauman's shoes were size 6, and the pair in hand at Christie's were 5B. She asked Schreiber to pass along any information that might help.

The Christie's agent also made her own attempts to verify authenticity, but apparently with little success. On July 29, 1981, she composed a letter of thanks to Schreiber:

> Dear Susan:
>
> I thought by this time I might have some additional information to pass along, but I've really come up blank. I tried to contact the shoe manufacturer who made the shoes (to see if they could tell me exactly how many pairs were made), but after two weeks of following false leads, I finally concluded that they're no longer in existence. There are several shoe stores in Los Angeles with that name, but evidently there's no connection to the original store.
>
> The man who consigned the shoes worked for MGM, and he has a theory about the variations in shoe size. He says MGM bought several pairs of a mass manufactured pump (which they covered with sequined chiffon themselves) and simply bought all the pairs that were even near Judy Garland's size when they located the style that met their specifications. In other words, they couldn't get them all in her size.
>
> Another theory could be that after dancing around all day under hot lights, she may have needed two or three different sizes! (Plus shoes for the stand-in.)
>
> Anyway, I'm enclosing a photo of our shoes and also one of the dress, which I thought you might like to see...

Among Susan Schreiber, Roberta Bauman and Julie Collier, there were no additional leads and the mystery remained. Years later, when I contacted Julie Collier at Christie's, she was still very curious about the disposition of the ruby slippers.

"There are several pairs in existence," she said. "We sold our pair — the size 5Bs — for $12,000 on October 1, 1981. They were painted red on the bottom and Judy Garland's name was inside on the lining. The Smithsonian also has a pair, and I think there's some lady who has a pair that she won in a contest two years after the movie was made. Ours were marked #7."

I had many questions for Collier, who maintained a professional air throughout our first conversation. I specifically wondered about provenance. Did Christie's ever question the legitimate ownership of the shoes they had auctioned? After all, the auctioneers maintained that one and only one pair of shoes was sold at MGM. "Not really," she answered. "We assume that all our clients come by their property legally. There was quite a lot of publicity surrounding the sale." However, she added, the consignor chose to remain anonymous. "In the auction business," she related, "owners are either proud of their possessions and want everyone to know or they're private people. We never divulge the names of buyers or consignors."

I said that I knew that the consignor had to be Kent Warner. People had already told me so, and the shoes Christie's had sold matched the description of the shoes that Leo said Kent had kept on display in his living room. Collier said the shoes were purchased by a family in Northern California who thought it would be fun to have them. It was an "impulsive purchase," she said.

When I asked about the condition of the slippers, she said, "The Smithsonian shoes are in the worst condition. Our pair were in better condition." She said that people had called her through the years and asked her to tell them anything she knew about the slippers. But she could not get beyond her own frustrations of trying to learn the truth of the multiple pairs of slippers. "It's so strange," she admitted. "Everyone's very secretive."

* * *

My own interest in *The Wizard of Oz* had been sparked years before my visit to the MGM script vault, when a University of California professor had touted L. Frank Baum's classic fairy tale as a "political parable on Populism." I accepted the idea immediately and started to pursue information that lent evidence to support the theory.

I only needed to look at the characters of *The Wizard of Oz* in the context of the time in which Baum wrote to find distinct similarities between the fairy tale and contemporary history. That was the beginning of my Kansas education...

Populism was a 19th century political phenomenon that rose out of the ruined, drought-plagued, money-poor grain belt of the Midwest. It rose like a tornado in the bleak black-and-white corn fields of Kansas, and swept into Chicago in 1896, where the Democratic Party nominated William Jennings Bryan for President.

As America expanded her waistband, adding girth and muscle with the railroads and settling of the nation, the working people of the Midwest — the small farmers of Kansas, Nebraska, the Dakotas, Missouri, Iowa, southern Illinois and Indiana, the merchants who built their stores and stocked them with seed and fertilizer, the sharecroppers who worked the fields — all found their world crumbling beneath a mountain of paper debt. It conspired like an evil wind of locusts to descend upon the green of the land and spoil it brown with dust.

And it was the worst in Kansas. A terrible winter and several seasons without rain had brought years of financial depression to Kansas while the rest of the country prospered. Farmers borrowed money against crops they could not produce and fell hopelessly into debt. Besides the rotten luck of the weather, the farmers blamed a tight national money supply for their troubles.

At the time, Uncle Sam banked on the "gold standard," which conservative Republican presidents such as Benjamin Harrison and William McKinley had called a "sound money" policy. The "gold standard" specified that a measure of gold be held in the vaults of Fort Knox for every dollar in circulation, setting an arbitrary limit on the real wealth of the nation.

To make matters worse, Grover Cleveland, a Democrat, had lowered the amount of the gold held in reserve and thus the amount of paper in circulation. Money became expensive. When the farmers recovered from the drought, they found their crops were abundant, but they were not commanding an equal share of the money supply. A bushel of Kansas corn cost more to grow than it was worth to sell.

Compounding that, railroads were in the practice of juggling freight rates to Chicago at harvest time. Fares went up during the weeks farmers most needed to ship their crops to the commodities markets. When a farmer couldn't pay for the rail, he blamed it on the price of his corn, and the price was already low because there wasn't enough money going around. Bryan's "Free Silver" became the cry of the land.

For every great cry there must be a voice and if ever there was a voice it was that of William Jennings Bryan. In 1896 the "Orator of the Platte" went to Chicago to deliver his "Cross of Gold" speech to Democratic Party conventioneers.

It was at this 1896 convention, said John Dos Passos, that "the minister's son whose lips had never touched liquor let out his silver voice so that it filled the gigantic hall, filled the ears of the plain people." He spoke to the "gold delegates" from the East, who filled their half of the hall with support for the incumbent, Grover Cleveland.

It's difficult to say how many farmers actually understood what "free silver" meant, but Bryan's oratory had them believing. Dos Passos wrote: "They roared their lungs out, carried Bryan round the hall on their shoulders, hugged him, loved him, named their children after him, nominated him for president, boy orator of the Platte, silver tongue of the plain people."

Bryan's powerful voice was heard from the corn fields of Kansas to the cornerstone of Wall Street. Political battle lines were drawn, not between Republicans and Democrats, but between those for "gold" and those for "silver." It was a classic American struggle between the have's and the have-not's.

The Eastern establishment insisted that the problems of the farmers had nothing to do with banking. If they would just turn out their crops profitably, like a business, they would be out of debt. It was the farmer's stupidity that made misfortune, not a system of banking. To this end, the Easterners influenced their friends in the press who depicted the Kansas farmer in cartoon caricature as a scarecrow, a man with hay for brains.

Such ridicule came home to roost in Kansas in August of 1896, when William Allen White, the young editor of the *Emporia Gazette* wrote "pure vitriol" about the plight of his state:

> "Go east and you hear them laugh at Kansas; go west and they sneer at her; go south and they cuss her; go north and they have forgotten her. Go into any crowd of intelligent people gathered anywhere on the globe, and you will find the Kansas man on the defensive. The newspaper columns and magazines once devoted to praise of her, to boastful facts and startling figures concerning her resources, are now filled with cartoons, jibes and Pefferian speeches. Kansas just naturally isn't in it. She has traded places with Arkansas and Timbuktu.
>
> "What's the matter with Kansas?"

What was the matter with Kansas, White said, was her people.

It was amidst this mælstrom of Populism that L. Frank Baum wrote *The Wizard of Oz*.

Baum's Scarecrow represented the Kansas farmer, made to feel dumb by the great Midwestern drought of the 1890s and low crop prices. "If I only had a brain," the Scarecrow laments, without knowing he already has the brain power he hopes to get from the Wizard.

The Tin Woodman was the victim of a "curse" cast by the Wicked Witch of the East. Her spell dehumanized labor; when he swung his ax, he chopped off a limb. The harder, faster and better he worked, the more he became like a machine. "If I only had a heart," he says, but his rusting tears display the goodness of a truly great heart.

The Cowardly Lion's great roar was heard throughout the Land of Oz, like Bryan's powerful "Cross of Gold" speech. But Bryan lost the election, and would go on to lose another, and another. He would never be President. The candidate, like the Cowardly Lion, could roar, but not win a fight. "If I only had the nerve," the lion complains. Yet his courage and bravery were often undeniable.

Dorothy brought these three characters together. She was Miss Everyperson, blessed with the kiss of the Good Witch, and wearing the charmed "silver shoes." She convinced the others that she was going to see the Great Wizard of Oz and that he would help her get back home to Kansas. She was sure the Wizard would also help her friends. She was sure because she believed.

But the great and powerful Wizard of Oz was, in his own words, "nothing but a bumbler, a humbug." He only had power because people, like Dorothy, believed he had power. Even the Witches of the East and West believed the Wizard had power. "Had they not thought I was more powerful than they themselves," the Wizard told Dorothy after she had found him out, "they would surely have destroyed me."

Was it coincidence that the Wicked Witch of the West, who threatened the Scarecrow — the farmer — with fire, should be killed by water? Bring rain to Kansas and the farmer profits. Baum's witches portrayed evil in popular forms — drought to the farmer, boss to the laborer, fear in the voice of the people.

These characterizations alone do not make a parable, but Baum's metallic metaphor does. When Dorothy begins her walk to the Emerald City, Baum describes "her silver shoes, tinkling merrily on the hard, yellow roadbed." Metal on metal, silver on gold.

Henry M. Littlefield, a high school teacher from Mount Vernon, New York, was the first to argue that Baum's *Oz* was a political parable, and stated that "the allegory is abundantly clear." He said Silver represented valid power in a land of make-believe, just as gold did on Wall Street. He said there was no mystery in Baum's Land of *Oz* — Big O, little z, the abbreviation for ounce. The silver shoes had the power, all Dorothy had to do was believe.

When the Wizard left the Emerald City in his balloon, he left Dorothy wondering how she would ever get home to Kansas. To Glinda, the Good Witch, she appealed. "Your silver shoes will carry you over the desert," Glinda told her. "If you had known their power you could have gone back to your Aunt Em the very first day you came to this county." And so Dorothy "clapped the heels of her shoes together three times, saying 'Take me home to Aunt Em.' "

Baum created a fairy tale with a Populist allegory. When Dorothy returns to Oz with the witch's broom, she learns that the Wizard is a meek little man. "Are you not a great Wizard?" she asks. The Wizard replies: "I have been making believe."

History has never been well served by Hollywood. When the producers of *The Wizard of Oz* changed Baum's silver slippers to ruby, they probably didn't care that they were tampering with a literary metaphor. They probably didn't give the slightest thought to Baum's *Oz* as a political parable on turn-of-the-century Populism; they didn't care about the historical importance of the silver shoes that they re-souled. No one could have understood that the ruby slippers they created would assume a mysterious, material charm of their own.

* * *

"THEY'RE MINE BY RIGHTS"

Roberta Bauman, the middle class mother of three, now living a simple life in Memphis, Tennessee, was the most unlikely character to be found in the middle of a Hollywood mystery. Born in the Roaring Twenties and reared during the Depression, she married during The War and raised her family in the 1950s. She liked to tell people that Elvis Presley went to *her* high school and she clearly was not ready for the onslaught of media attention that befell her after that exciting day in May, 1970.

Surprised by the attention, Roberta offered the press her only story about the ruby slippers: she had won them in a movie contest in 1940, and they measured size 6B. Her story made both the AP and UPI wire services and became a popular subject back in Los Angeles, where two local television stations did reports on her pair of the shoes, including one live broadcast from Roberta's living room by KABC-TV. It didn't take long for word to get back to Culver City. Even though Roberta's attempts to contact MGM had been unsuccessful — they hadn't even opened her letter — the costumers on the MGM lot that week were quite aware of her question.

Simply, Roberta wanted to know if her pair of ruby slippers were real. She couldn't get a straight answer. Rumor from the wardrobe department said the Southern lady's shoes had belonged to Garland's stand-in. Roberta did not hear this rumor for seven years.

It began shortly after the auction, in the days after it was announced in the papers that there was more than one pair of ruby slippers. Under the laws of liquidation, auctioneer David Weisz would have been required to divulge knowledge of any other pairs, if he knew for certain that any existed. When the auction pair sold for $15,000, the buyer had assumed he'd purchased the one and only pair of ruby slippers.

Costumers at MGM agreed that the guy was a bit of a fool for not knowing what he was buying. Among themselves they admitted that there had to be other pairs; but when asked by David Weisz, they could only say that the shoes had "disappeared." Nobody really knew what had happened, except Kent Warner. He must have laughed when he heard about Roberta's shoes. They belonged to the stand-in, he told friends, because they were so big. Judy Garland had a small foot, he convinced those who asked. Based on his experience in the business, Warner's argument was generally accepted.

In 1977, when Aljean Harmetz published *The Making of The Wizard of Oz,* she wrote about the auction of the ruby slippers:

> "Judy Garland had worn size 4B shoes and the auctioned slippers were labeled 4B. Debbie Reynolds, who also wears a 4, insisted that the auctioned slippers were too big for her and thus must have belonged to Garland's stand-in. The stand-in, Bobbie Koshay, wore size 6; and Mrs. Henry Bauman of Memphis, Tennessee, displayed a pair of 'Judy Garland's red shoes' — size 6B — that she had won in a contest in 1939."

Of all the press Roberta received after announcing the existence of her slippers, none was more damaging than this. By simple reasoning, anyone could figure that Roberta's shoes belonged to Judy Garland's stand-in.

Roberta didn't believe this, for one good reason: "Back in those days when I was given the ruby slippers, you believed what you were told by those old schoolmarms. Those ladies were tough. If they saw you walking down the hall with your arm around a boy, they'd karate chop it off. When they told you something, you'd better believe it was the truth." Roberta clung to her belief, but the question nagged her mind: "Could Miss Josephine have been misled too?"

Roberta wasn't the only one talking to herself after reading Harmetz's book. The inference that the auctioned pair had also belonged to Garland's stand-in raised the eyebrows of David Weisz, the "Southern California millionaire," and, eventually, curators at the Smithsonian. Nobody could really be sure. Facts were not what they appeared to be.

Something Harmetz wrote made me wonder if she really knew the absolute truth. She got wrong the date that Roberta received her ruby slippers. It was not 1939, but 1940. That alone was a clue. I had to examine more carefully her dialectical argument in which she leapt from conclusion to conclusion, which led me to question the major premise of her thesis: Did Judy Garland wear size 4B shoes?

Jeanette MacDonald wore a size 4B, and Kent Warner found many pairs of her shoes in the dusty MGM storage bins. One costumer who was there described those shoes as "incredibly small," considerably smaller than Judy Garland's ruby shoes.

At the auction, even Debbie Reynolds had claimed that she wore the same size shoe as Judy Garland, as Harmetz wrote. The auctioned shoes were "too big" for Debbie's feet, but that wasn't positive proof that Judy Garland wore a 4B.

My first bit of evidence came from a newspaper article, dated November 4, 1978, which reported the scheduled auction of "Judy Garland's treasures." According to the *San Francisco Chronicle* article, by the syndicated New York columnist Suzy Knickerbocker, the C.B. Charles Galleries were selling a number of Garland possessions at the Beverly Wilshire Hotel in Beverly Hills.

They were selling Judy's letters from the Duchess of Windsor, Bing Crosby, Maurice Chevalier, Ali Kahn, Jack Benny, Joan Crawford, John Foster Dulles and others. They were selling her reading glasses and her custom-made golf clubs, makeup cases and several scrapbooks. They also sold dozens of her *size 6-1/2 B shoes.*

An unexpecting Dorothy tries on a new pair of shoes.

L. Frank Baum, author of The Wizard of Oz, *circa 1908.*

Ruby Slippers as displayed at the Smithsonian Institution until 1988. Display has recently been changed. Plaque reads: "Ruby slippers worn by Judy Garland (Frances Gumm) in 1939 MGM film The Wizard of Oz.*"*

1939 title card for The Wizard of Oz.

Screenwriter Noel Langley, credited with changing Dorothy's "Silver Shoes" to "Ruby Slippers." Circa 1939

CONTINUED (2)   26

                North Witch (to Dorothy)
Tell her to find out for herself.

                West Witch
Aha! Then you did!

                Dorothy (anxiously)
Quite by accident --

                West Witch
Accident! You kill my ~~dearest friend and severest critic~~ and then pass it off as an accident, do you?
Well, you're not the only one that can cause accidents!
                (she raises her broomstick in the air)
So can I!

CLOSE SHOT - NORTH WITCH - DOROTHY
                North Witch (quickly)
Just a minute!
                (she waves her wand)

C.U. ~~SILVER~~ Ruby SHOES

sticking out from under the house. They vanish.

C.U. DOROTHY'S FEET
The ~~silver~~ ruby shoes appear on Dorothy's feet, ~~glittering~~ sparkling in the sun.

MED. SHOT - NORTH WITCH, DOROTHY, WEST WITCH
                West Witch (screaming) (landing her broomstick on the ground)
Give me those shoes! Please - please give me those
shoes - they're mine by rights - please give them
to me!!
                North Witch (to Dorothy)
You keep right inside them - they're magic. Now
she can't do anything to you unless she gets you
into her own country; so as long as you keep away
from the West of Oz, you can snap your fingers
under her nose!

CLOSE SHOT - WEST WITCH
                West Witch (snarling) you would busybody!
Curse you ~~for~~ meddling, I'll
reckon with you later for that!
                                CONTINUED:

Page from Noel Langley's May 14, 1938 OZ script showing historic Hollywood decision.

OZ costume designer, Adrian, as seen in 1929 with Greta Garbo.

Dorothy, sporting a new pair of Ruby slippers, takes her first step on The Yellow Brick Road.

Test photo of Judy Garland wearing "Arabian test shoes" and the "Bugle bead shoes."
Arabian shoes are in the collection of Debbie Reynolds.

Western Costume shoemaker Joe Napoli, credited by some as the maker of the Ruby Slippers.

Publicity still from first two weeks of OZ shooting under director Richard Thorpe.
Note Dorothy's blonde hair and Ruby Slippers without bows.

When Judy's feet were not featured in a scene, she preferred wearing a different kind of slipper.

Ruby Slippers as displayed before sale at the MGM auction in 1970.
This pair sold for $15,000 and eventually went to the Smithsonian Institution.

Roberta Bauman displays her pair of Ruby Slippers the morning after another pair sold for $15,000 at the MGM auction, much to the surprise of all concerned.

Announcement of the 1970 MGM auction exhibition, outside Lot 2 at the MGM Studio in Culver City.

Senior class photo of William Bowden, taken in 1940. The year he received the gavel used by Harry Carey in Mr. Smith Goes to Washington

Roberta Jeffries Bauman as seen in 1940, the year she received a pair of Ruby Slippers as her "Hollywood Prize."

Clark Gable's "lucky" trenchcoat as displayed for the MGM star wardrobe sale on Stage 27, next to Ingrid Bergman's costume from Gaslight.

EDDIE FISHER

Costumes displayed on MGM Stage 27 for MGM star wardrobe 1970 auction preview.
Kent Warner set up most of the display.

EDDIE FISHER

Feature costume display as built by Kent Warner for the 1970 MGM auction.
In foreground is one of ten "Dorothy" dresses worn by Judy Garland in OZ.

Costume designed by Adrian for Norma Shearer in Marie Antoinette *(1938).*

Title card for 1949 re-release of OZ.

Protruding feet of the recently squished Wicked Witch of the East, shortly before she loses her shoes. Slipper fanatics will note a higher heel than on shoes worn by Judy Garland in the film.

Kent Warner's personal pair of Ruby Slippers, marked "#7 Judy Garland," in preview photo before being auctioned by Christie's East in 1981. The "Witch's" shoes.

Actress Debbie Reynolds, as seen on the day of the MGM "Star Wardrobe" auction in 1970.

Kent Warner preparing the MGM Star Wardrobe display just days before the auction in 1970.

I found the second clue in conversation with a woman who had purchased a pair of Judy Garland shoes for $200. They were a pair of black velvet pumps, size 5C, worn by Garland in *A Star Is Born*.

I couldn't be certain, but my instincts were still with Roberta Bauman. Others said I had forgotten that Judy Garland was a growing girl when she made *The Wizard of Oz*, and then again, Judy herself said she was chubby. The best I knew was that two pairs of ruby slippers definitely existed, sized 5C and 6B. Kent Warner was rumored to have had another pair, sized 5B. Maybe more. Only by finding other pairs could the truth be revealed.

Harmetz was dead right when she said "what happened to every pair of the ruby slippers is not clear, but at least two pairs were stolen from the wardrobe department." But if she knew this, how did she miss Kent Warner's name?

Harmetz made the most provocative claim of all when she wrote that "late in 1974, Debbie Reynolds was offered one of those stolen pairs for her museum."

Reynolds clearly wanted a pair of Judy Garland's ruby slippers for the proposed museum. Her first opportunity to buy a pair came before the MGM auction. According to Richard Carroll, Reynolds approached David Weisz about donating the ruby slippers to the museum. Weisz wouldn't make a donation, but what Reynolds didn't know was that he might have considered selling them to the actress, quite privately. Other people, such as Jack Haley, Jr., were afforded this privilege by Weisz and MGM studio president James Aubrey. Apparently, Reynolds didn't ask Weisz if he would consider a price.

Although Reynolds, by her own admission, borrowed $100,000 to buy MGM auction memorabilia, she said she didn't have any of the money left when it came time to buy the slippers. Reynolds did not make a single bid for the ruby slippers, though she sat in the audience when they were auctioned. If Harmetz is correct, perhaps Reynolds didn't bid because she didn't think the slippers were worn by Garland. But is it possible that Reynolds knew something the public didn't? Did she know there were other pairs of ruby slippers? Of

course. Eventually she would get her pair. And she would get them
from Kent Warner.

* * *

GOWNS, by ADRIAN

Given the existence of at least two pairs of ruby slippers — Roberta Bauman's pair, and those sold at the MGM auction, which were subsequently donated to the Smithsonian — the search for other pairs inevitably took me back to the beginning. If I could establish how many pairs had been made, it would be easier to determine how many might still exist. But tracing the source of their creation only fueled the mystery.

"It was in Mrs. Cluett's Beading Department that Judy Garland's ruby slippers were made," wrote Aljean Harmetz in *The Making of The Wizard of Oz,* the definitive study of MGM's Production No. 1060. Harmetz's work is constantly quoted in articles about the ruby slippers, with and without attribution, but does not answer the crucial question of how many.

From the moment it was decided that Dorothy would wear ruby, not silver-colored, shoes, their provenance fell into the able hands of Louis B. Mayer's flamboyant couturier, Gilbert Adrian.

Known best by only his surname, Adrian first sketched the ruby slippers during the summer of 1938. While they were the most important shoes in the movie, they certainly were not the foremost costumes on the designer's mind. He was terribly preoccupied with more than 100 different Munchkin outfits, which consumed his passionate imagination for wardrobe design.

Production was slated to begin October 12, 1938, and by that time Adrian had ordered ruby slippers to be made in two distinct styles. The first was a wildly jeweled, Arabian affair, with curling toes and heels. They must have looked great on the protruding feet of the dead

Wicked Witch, but not so hot on Dorothy. On Judy Garland, the shoes did not quite fit the Kansas farm girl image that producer Mervyn LeRoy intended to put on the screen. They belonged in the Sahara Desert, not in the corn fields of America. This design came to be known as the "Arabian test pair."

The second ruby slipper style seemed much more reasonable: a basic schoolgirl pump, with a short, French heel. These shoes were ornately covered with rhinestones and bugle beads, and were distinct from future pairs, in that they had no bows. They were known as the "bugle bead shoes." During the first two weeks of photography, when director Richard Thorpe was still on the job, Garland wore the "bugle bead" shoes.

Shortly before Halloween, Thorpe was tossed off the picture and George Cukor was brought in to resurrect producer LeRoy's original cinematic intentions. During this time, Adrian probably realized the final design of the ruby slippers. He added a bow, and determined that the shoes should be covered with sequins. This design was tested for color and appearance on Halloween, 1938, along with other costumes and hairstyles for the assorted characters. This ruby slipper suited everyone's needs; it photographed well under exceedingly bright lights, and could be easily reproduced.

For continuity, Garland would need more than one pair of ruby slippers. She would need slippers for walking, skipping, standing, dancing, running, touching and tapping. Because the slippers carried the movie's central theme, Adrian wouldn't have been caught dead on the set of Stage 27 without a mint pair of ruby slippers for every scene. Garland made this difficult because, on her feet, the shoes took a terrible beating. They would have to make many pairs of ruby slippers, not just doubles and triples.

"They," according to Western Costume Company retiree Al Di-Pardo, were not the ladies of the MGM wardrobe department, as Harmetz suggested, but a Western Costume cobbler named Joe Napoli. "Joe Napoli made the ruby slippers," said DiPardo with a voice that was sandpaper smooth.

"I worked at Western Costume for 39 years," DiPardo said, "from 1937 to 1976. I was 21, a cutter. The ruby slippers were made from original red satin shoes. They had a baby French heel, a *spool* heel, one and a half inches. Just a regular pair of pumps. Nothing but a slipper, a pump. They were very simple to duplicate."

How many pairs did Napoli make, I asked? "I don't know," DiPardo laughed. "Quite a few."

"They were just another pair of shoes," said Robert Niewoehner, another retired employee of Western, who recalled Napoli making the shoes. "There are several pairs, you know." I knew. "I employed Joe Napoli," Niewoehner said. "Joe was in charge of the shoe department. We were the only shop making costume shoes back then, the only ones in town. The ruby slippers weren't important then. It was just another show. But not anymore. Now it's all out of whack."

Sally Nelson Harb, the resident historian at Western Costume, verified that both DiPardo and Nieworhner had worked for the company and confirmed DiPardo's story, which she double-checked with company president, John Golden. Sadly, the giant costume house had no records concerning the making of the shoes.

DiPardo remembered when Judy Garland came in to be fitted. "We had her footprint and her last," he said. "Her foot was very thin." I wondered if those records still existed, but DiPardo didn't know. "I think they pulled them. Mr. Golden always had us pull the footprint and the last when a star died. I definitely remember pulling Marilyn Monroe and Walt Disney. Mr. Golden took them. But Judy Garland... " DiPardo thought. "I don't know."

A quick check at Western revealed that all the shoe department records had been destroyed during the 1970s, when the shop was consolidated for space. The Garland footprints, which had been carefully filed by Joe Napoli and then Al Dipardo, were no longer there. But along the longest wall of the shoe shop, lasts still existed. From floor to ceiling, covering the length of the room, these lasts — the wooden molds a shoemaker used to build a shoe — were stashed. Could Judy Garland's ruby slippers' last be there?

Mauricio Osorio, Western's cobbler when I visited, said yes. And from the wall he produced a last, size 6-1/2B. Around this last, which was marked with the size and the number 150, the ruby slipper sequin overlay could have been produced, along with many other pairs of Judy Garland shoes. But, Osorio could find no proof. "This was her last," he said, "but there could have been others."

Were the ruby slippers made at MGM, or at Western Costume? Harmetz quoted two women who worked in MGM's wardrobe department. One, Vera Mordaunt, recalled that "they tested many shoes. They must have tried five or six ways to make the shoes. I think the final shoes were satin. They were definitely some kind of cloth. The chiffon with the sequins was formed in the shape of a shoe and then sewed onto the cloth shoe."

Marian Parker, Harmetz wrote, "remembers the sequins themselves as being glued onto the chiffon rather than sewn." Further testimonial, Harmetz said, came from Roger Mayer, who could not imagine that the studio would farm out work of this nature. Yet Al DiPardo and Robert Niewoehner distinctly remembered Western making the shoes.

I spoke with Harmetz and neither of us could be certain of any fact, except that over time, memories do fade. I concluded that the slippers must have been made in *both* places.

MGM probably made the test pairs which were used while director Richard Thorpe spent his 12 days shooting scenes that would later be scrapped. In all his footage, most of which was thrown away, Judy Garland was wearing a pair of ruby slippers without bows. This must have been the "bugle bead" pair.

When Thorpe was fired, many of the costumes were changed, including Dorothy's gingham dress and ruby slippers. The costumers and seamstresses no doubt recognized the enormity of their task to outfit all the wildly costumed characters for the movie and certainly were overworked. They were already busy with more than a hundred Munchkins, flying monkeys, and other assorted and fantastically dressed extras, along with the Lion, Scarecrow and Tin Woodman costumes. They may not have had time to make all the ruby slippers.

The fresh start also gave Adrian time to stabilize the entire wardrobe and with so many costumes to worry about, he couldn't spend much time worrying about the ruby shoes. With their design settled, he probably commissioned the making of several pairs for continuous use in the movie.

Nobody knows how many "continuity" pairs of ruby slippers were ordered in the Fall of 1938. MGM lost those records long ago. Quite typically, nobody considered them important history. Chances are, Adrian did not anticipate Judy Garland's needing as many pairs of ruby slippers as were eventually made; they may have been manufactured in waves. My guess was that the continuity shoes were made at Western Costume.

Further indication that the construction of the ruby slippers was done in different quarters came from a gentleman named Eddie Fisher, who worked in the MGM leather room in 1938. Fisher related that he and co-worker Nick Samson were given the job of producing bows for the ruby slippers.

"Two weeks before shooting began," Fisher said, "two young men from the wardrobe department came to the leather room. They opened two shoe boxes and placed on the work bench two pairs of red slippers with bows of red silk ribbons. They said Adrian had made a last minute change on the bows and showed us a sketch by Adrian of an entirely different kind of bow...

"The sketch showed a leather bow shaped somewhat like butterfly wings that lay flat on the shoes and implanted around the edges were red rhinestones. In the center were three raised red stones that glittered like jewels, and between the edges and the red stones were implanted bugles.

"At a glance one could see by the sketch this new bow, or buckle as Nick and I called it, was a great improvement over the red silk ribbon bows. We were requested to make four pairs of identical bows as shown by the sketch.

"We took a section of good grained 1/8-inch leather and dyed it a bright red. With our leather tools we made all those indentations of a pattern from the sketch. Next we painstakingly implanted all those rhinestones, bugle beads, and red stones in the center that were supplied by wardrobe.

"After completion of our work we called wardrobe and one of the young men came and picked up one pair. He said Adrian wanted to see them. He later returned with the pair of slippers and said Adrian was pleased and complimented our work. He also said both pairs were to be left at the leather room until called for.

"The day before shooting began, a different wardrobe person came to the leather room and asked for the shoes. We set both boxes with the slippers before him. He said he would only take one pair as the second pair would be safer left with us than at wardrobe."

Fisher gave the wardrobe man one pair of shoes and two extra bows, then put the second pair of slippers on a shelf. Wardrobe didn't call for the second pair, Fisher said, for five months, when just four days remained on the *Oz* shooting schedule.

"Another different wardrobe person came to the leather room with the original first pair of slippers that Judy Garland had worn during that time, requesting that we re-sole them in a hurry. The sole of the left shoe had a hole the size of a small finger just paper thin of being through."

Nick Samson, Fisher said, gave the wardrobe man the pair of new slippers he had on the shelf. "The wardrobe person seemed surprised that there was a second pair." Still, the first pair was left for repair, but because so few days of shooting remained, Samson didn't do the work. Instead, Fisher explained, Samson put the old pair in the box, marked *Oz* on the end, and put it back on the shelf.

"No one ever came from wardrobe to pick up that first pair of slippers," Fisher said. There they remained for thirty years.

The slippers cost about $15 to make in 1938, but would undergo considerable alterations, including a layer of orange felt to muffle the sound of the leather soles on the plywood Yellow Brick Road. Certainly, different pairs of shoes were used for different filming needs, wide shots, close-ups, inserts. Shoes for walking, standing, skipping, dancing, running, touching and tapping. Fisher said he and Nick Samson made only four sets of bows, but there could have been as many as seven pairs of ruby slippers. But how many?

One thing was certain: the intricate beading and stitching, combined with the materials of the day, make Judy Garland's ruby slippers genuine period pieces. They may have been easy to duplicate in 1938, as Al DiPardo maintained, but not fifty years later.

With principal photography completed in March, 1939, *The Wizard of Oz* wardrobe ensemble was packed into the burgeoning MGM costume closet. Chances are, wardrobe department personnel kept the collection intact until the film was "in the can." This insured continuity should the producers want to re-shoot or insert a scene into the movie. After that, the wardrobe was "broken down."

In a world of normal costumes, this meant that all the men's belts would be stored with other men's belts in the Men's Wardrobe department, blouses with blouses in Ladies Wardrobe, shirts with shirts, suits with suits, gowns with gowns, and shoes with shoes. Divided by gender and catalogued by garment, everything would be re-used.

But *Oz* costumes were anything but normal. To MGM costumers, the wardrobe presented re-use problems. Certain pieces, such as the witches' costumes worn by Margaret Hamilton and Billie Burke, were applicable to a few other films. But how often do Munchkins and flying monkeys appear in movies? Also, the costumes were so distinct that they would be easily recognized in other films; this was especially true of the Lion's pelt, the Strawman and Tin Woodman suits, Dorothy's gingham dress and the ruby slippers. Most of the *Oz* costumes were put in MGM's form of deep storage.

What happened to all the ruby slippers after production stopped is anybody's guess. One pair definitely went to New York in the Fall of 1939, where they were used to promote the movie (probably on the feet of a life-size Dorothy doll). That pair became Roberta

Bauman's "Hollywood prize" and were sent the following February to Memphis, Tennessee.

Mickey Carroll, one of the 32 surviving Munchkins, told a story about "Toto," Dorothy's dog, eating one of the ruby slippers in Judy Garland's dressing room. Jack Haley, Jr. recalled that a set of *Oz* effigies, representing Dorothy and friends, was costumed by the wardrobe department in 1948 and sent out on a tour promoting the theatrical re-release of the movie. Nothing, he said, came back.

Eddie Fisher said one pair of the slippers remained in MGM's leather room until 1974, when everything there was trashed.

What actually became of the rest? They were probably consigned to a wardrobe storage room, where they remained, untouched, for thirty years.

* * *

"...KANSAS, SHE SAYS, IS THE NAME OF THE STAR"

"**A**ll right, Miss Smarty, you didn't behave tonight so I'm leaving you forever."

With that pronouncement, Ethel Gumm left her ten-year-old daughter, Frances, sitting on the bed in a fleabag hotel room in a small town in Oregon.

"I sat on that bed all night and cried," Frances said. "It happened several times." Little Frances Gumm didn't have much of a child-hood.

> *Somewhere*
> *Over The Rainbow*
> *way up high*
> *There's a*
> *land that I heard of*
> *once in a lullaby*

She had made her debut at the age of two, dashing on stage at the New Grand Theater in Grand Rapids, Minnesota, on amateur night. She was a little girl with a big voice. She stole the spotlight from her sisters, Mary Jane and Virginia, singing *Jingle Bells,* until her father swooped her up in his arms and carried her off before she could begin the song for an eighth time.

The Gumm sisters formed an act, which made Chicago vaudeville in 1931, where they opened for George Jessel. Legend had it that the marquee was misspelled reading: "The Glum Sisters."

Jessel suggested a name change, to avoid the dreadful mala-
propism. Something like *Garland*, he said, the last name of a drama
critic in New York City. "The Garland Sisters" they became, and soon
their act was reviewed by *Variety*: "The youngest handles ballads like
a veteran and gets every word and note over with a personality that
hits audiences. Her sisters merely form a backdrop."

> *Somewhere over the rainbow*
> *skies are blue*
> *And the dreams*
> *that you dare to dream*
> *really do come true*

The little girl with the big voice came to Hollywood, her mother
as always the driving force. She had driven the back roads and high-
ways across a struggling nation, from town to city where "The Garland Sisters" would play. They sang in back room theaters where a
night's pay covered a night's stay and a morning meal and maybe
enough gas to get to the next show. This time her mother drove Frances to play a four-a-day house in Los Angeles. It was the right place
in time.

In *Pigskin Parade* she appeared with Betty Grable and Patsy Kelly,
and first met the Tin Woodman, Jack Haley. Then Louis B. Mayer
took sight, and sound, of the ingenue. The man gave the little girl with
the big voice a healthy studio contract. Then he made her star.

Somewhere over the rainbow could have been a place where
young Judy Garland often wished to be. Mayer crammed her into
seven pictures in two years, all the while building her star image with
his army of publicists. The reality of her life had to fit the movie
dream. When *Love Finds Andy Hardy* appeared, Judy was given a
tabloid crush on Mickey Rooney and the studio arranged for them to
be seen together at every photo opportunity. Mayer made her image,
but Judy made Dorothy.

Some day I'll wish upon a star
and wake up where the clouds are far
behind me
Where troubles melt like lemon drops
away above the chimney tops
that's where you'll find me

If not for the usual twist of fate, Judy Garland might never have starred as Dorothy. But she did. It was a role she loved: "I loved the music and I loved the director... and of course I loved the story."

It was also a role she hated: "I don't know why they didn't go out and find a girl that looked like Dorothy instead of bending me out of shape for the part. I was a chubby little girl, so they'd truss me up in a corset so I couldn't sing very well. They put caps on my teeth. They starved me to lose weight. They even put stuff in my nose to make it look different.

"I played little Dorothy Gale of Kansas in that picture, but I was tortured little Tillie during the whole damned thing."

In exchange for her childhood, Mayer gave her everything a big money contract could buy, including her own dressing room, and a psychiatrist.

"No wonder I was strange. Imagine whipping out of bed, dashing over to the doctor's office, lying down on a torn leather couch, telling my troubles to an old man who couldn't hear, who answered with an accent I couldn't understand, and then dashing to Metro to make movie love to Mickey Rooney."

Movie making went on for 12, 14, 16 hours a day, with actors in makeup, in wardrobe, in the dressing room waiting, waiting, waiting under hot lights on stage for that fleeting moment of action. Boredom and slap-silly exhaustion brought on despair. Then she'd have to do a scene again. The little girl with the big voice would fall asleep making movies, making money for the patriotic man. To Louis B. Mayer, stars were manufactured, stars were machines.

"They'd take us to the studio hospital and knock us cold with sleeping pills... after four hours they'd wake us up and give us pep pills again. That's the way we worked and that's the way we got thin. That's the way we got mixed up. And that's the way we lost contact."

She went through pills and husbands and bottles of alcohol, but the tragedy of her life absorbed her fans. Garland came late to sets, hours, sometimes days after her call. She puffed up with water-fat, then lost too much weight. In 1950, at the age of 28, she slashed her throat after MGM suspended her contract. "I'm in a blizzard," she said.

Frances Gumm never learned to cope with Judy Garland; they merely co-existed. When she died, in London, on June 22, 1969, nobody was really surprised. Vincent Canby simply wondered "how she survived as long as she did." Her fragile heart could not keep beating the legend. Her legend, her star, grew bigger and brighter than the little girl with the big voice ever dared to dream her star could be.

> *Somewhere over the rainbow*
> > *bluebirds fly*
> > > *Birds fly over the rainbow*
> *Why then, oh why can't I?*

* * *

"A HORSE OF A DIFFERENT COLOR"

With the coming of the 50th anniversary of the release of *The Wizard of Oz*, MGM, in association with the Turner Entertainment Co., authorized the Franklin Mint to produce and sell a number of *Oz* collectibles, including an "official portrait doll" of Judy Garland as Dorothy.

"She's completely authentic," boasted an advertisement that appeared in many magazines, "even her ruby slippers." The only problem was that the Franklin Mint forgot to put bows on its version of Dorothy's magical shoes.

Tod Machin noticed. His name had come up in so many different conversations that I decided I should give him a call to find out what he knew about the slippers. The 28-year-old worked as an illustrator for the *Kansas City Star*, but his thoughts often drifted far away, to the Land of *Oz*. This was where he placed his heart.

Tod's interest in the ruby slippers began as a child. He said he "can't remember" when his interest in the movie *The Wizard of Oz* and the slippers "wasn't there."

During the early 1980s, his fascination developed into full-blown fanaticism; he became obsessed with the ruby slippers. He steadfastly sought information by writing letters to owners of ruby slippers — Roberta Bauman and the Smithsonian — and to Julie Collier at Christie's. People began to consider him somewhat of a slipper expert.

When the Franklin Mint offered its Dorothy doll, Tod immediately mailed his check for $135 and received his merchandise in the mail. He was duly impressed.

"They shaped her ankles very well," he said, "but forgot the bow." How did he know? "Those bottom twelve inches are very important to me," he calmly answered.

Through his own interest, Machin eventually built his own pair of ruby slippers. Using photographs provided by the Smithsonian, Christie's and Roberta Bauman, he constructed a pair of replicas that he described as "definitely good."

I asked a hypothetical question: "If your replicas were on display at the Smithsonian, how many of the five million visitors a year would recognize them as phonies?"

Tod pondered the question, then answered that, maybe, fifty people—one out of every hundred thousand—would know the difference.

"That," he said, "is no measure of my craftsmanship. Everybody knows what they are, but people are just basically ignorant as to what the shoes actually look like."

* * *

The foundation of each ruby slipper was a basic pump, purchased from the Innes Shoe Company of Los Angeles, Pasadena and Hollywood. Every authentic pair of ruby slippers has the Innes name, either a stitched white label with red-and-black lettering, or an embossed stamp in silver or gold. The name is prominent on the sole of the lining inside the right shoe of each pair. The shoes were covered with red satin and lined with cream-colored kid leather. To this shoe, the sequins were added.

The sequins were first stitched in rows onto a gabardine overlay, cut in the pattern of the shoe. This sequin-covered overlay was then sewn directly to each shoe, the thread snaking all the way through to the leather lining.

The fish-scale sequins were 3/16th of an inch round, and unique to their day in that they were reasonably thick and not dimpled in the center. Each shoe was covered with approximately 2,300 of these sequins. Because of the rigors of color-testing, all the shoes had to be dyed a deep crimson red so that they would appear to be ruby-colored, not orange, on the Technicolor film. Consequently, the ruby slippers are much darker in real life than they appear on the screen. Strangely, I learned, different pairs of ruby slippers come in different shades of ruby red, from bright to dark burgundy.

* * *

Tod's interest in the slippers and his membership in various *Oz* clubs and associations put him in contact with a number of *Oz* fans. When people learned that he had been collecting information and photographs of the shoes, they sometimes called him. This exposure introduced Tod to a fellow from North Carolina named Jack Townsend. From Tod, Townsend asked for close-up photos of the slippers for the purpose of making his own replicas. It wasn't until later that Tod learned that Townsend was selling his mock-ups.

Townsend advertised his shoes in *Film Collector's World*, a trade magazine for collectors, for a price of $250 and sold as many as six different pairs. Bob Tamkin of Los Angeles bought one of the sets. Tamkin was very impressed by Townsend's sincerity and craftsmanship, which included a detailed *Innes* label inside the right shoe. They were very close to authentic. The label was actually a photograph of the label in Roberta Bauman's pair of slippers. Townsend got the photo from Tod.

For my purposes, the information was valuable. It meant that there were replicas on the market that were very, very good. What did I learn? Buyer beware.

* * *

"WE'RE OFF TO SEE THE WIZARD"

By his accent people could tell that Kent Phillip Warner was from New York, where he was born on March 8, 1943. During a long interview in January, 1977, Kent told Los Angeles Times reporter Kathleen Hendrix that he came from a broken family; his parents had split when he was a baby. Until his mother remarried, Kent lived with his grandparents. For ten years, he said, he endured "kind of a dull and unhappy childhood."

His grandfather apparently took the boy in with misgivings, and Kent recalled no fond memories of the man: "He belittled everything I did. I should be a real mental case, a psychotic. If I tried to play ball with other kids, he'd belittle me in front of them, tell me what a screwup I was, so that I didn't want to play ball. I turned more and more to fantasy."

Where his grandfather's imagination stopped, his grandmother's imagination began. "I love her," he said. "She celebrated her 50th anniversary by divorcing my grandfather and marrying the man she'd been seeing for 25 years!" By indulging his fantasies, she introduced him to the refinements of a more gracious age, befitting a polished gentleman, not a street rowdy.

"On Saturday afternoons," Kent said, "she'd put on her best, put me in a suit, take me on a double-decker bus down Fifth Avenue to a good restaurant, show me how to use napkins and silver properly — it was just like Auntie Mame on a lower-middle class scale. She'd take me to matinees. We couldn't afford good tickets, but she put me onto the theater. God bless her for it."

Kent was fascinated by the theater and soon, with the advent of long-playing phonograph records, promoted his imagination by purchasing original cast albums, memorizing their music and lyrics, and reproducing each show on a miniature stage. He'd build a little set complete with figures and costumes, "do the lights, then move the figures around as the record went on. I'd relive the show in my mind."

George M. Cohan was one of Kent's favorites, and it was such shows as *The Yankee Doodle Boy* and *Give My Regards To Broadway* that introduced him, at an early age, to a world of "sweet band" music, to the Jazz and Swing eras of the 1930s and 1940s.

Into that world he retreated. Through fantasy he quenched his thirst for nostalgia, days he'd never known, "for something," he said, "I could just sort of hold onto as my very own."

At first he collected old 78s, thousands of them, but he also kept an eye toward telephones, radios, phonographs and even old clothes. Everywhere he went, Kent looked to the past and brought home reminders he could cherish.

A sign of the future came one rainy Saturday afternoon, a day he would never forget. An old widow had opened the attic of her huge Long Island estate to young Kent, and there he found clothes she had purchased in Paris, dating from the 1930s back to the turn of the century. He found designs by Lanvin, Patou, Worth and Chanel.

"I dragged them home, and my mother said 'what the hell are you going to do with all that?' I enjoyed looking at them, feeling them. I never wore them! I know a lot of people will think that's what I did."

* * *

Through fantasy, Warner found show business. After high school graduation, he tinkered with the thought of acting, but soon realized his bedroom stage show talent did not translate to the big picture. His mother, ever practical, encouraged her son to think about work in one of the entertainment's satellite businesses.

According to Warner, she said, "Listen, your Uncle Irving is in the catering business and makes a lot of money. You're going to go to Community College and learn about the catering business."

He did, but not for long. Several months into the course, the instructor brought into class "a cow's head with all the fur on it and a big fish with the eyes staring out of it. I was supposed to demonstrate cutting it all up for the rest of the class. That was it. I walked out." And into the costuming business.

Kent took a low-paying job with one of New York's older costume houses, Eaves, which supplied wardrobes to many theatrical productions. To his surprise, he found many costumes on their racks that reminded him of Saturday afternoons with his grandmother. Amidst these garments of his past, he found a home, but it was not in New York. Home was to be in Hollywood.

* * *

"I HAVE A FEELING WE'RE NOT IN KANSAS ANYMORE"

Kent loved Hollywood. Not the place, but the idea. His image of Hollywood was probably formed long before he ever moved to Los Angeles, by the movies of his childhood, the glamor and glitz of a world he had watched on black-and-white TV. Hollywood was a big production under hot lamps with men and women of action, adventure, drama, laughs, music and romance, swarming like bees in a fit of creation for the benefit of the camera's eye, making from the madness a moment of magic, like honeycomb from which the viewer could feed. He watched these movies, absorbed the moments, and imagined himself a part of the scene. For Kent, Hollywood was the place to be.

Sometime near his twenty-first birthday, Kent came to Hollywood. The world he found was not quite that of his dreams. Getting into the film business was not easy, but his New York credentials got him a job at Berman's Costume House in Los Angeles, where he started in June, 1964, at $72.50 a week.

At the time, Berman's, which competed with Western Costume, was big enough to support entire productions, had departments of clothing for men and ladies, and specialized in period pieces. It was at Berman's that Kent first saw the tattered threads from his favorite Hollywood movies.

Soon after Kent's hiring, the old RKO Studio in Hollywood — famous in the 1930s as the home of Fred Astaire and Ginger Rogers — was sold by Desilu, its owner since the 1950s, to Paramount. The rumor was that they were burning everything to clear out storage rooms.

Berman's, rather than see the collection destroyed, quietly purchased the RKO wardrobe. Kent was one of the first Berman employees to go to RKO to see what was there. He had to be shocked. Many
costumes were on racks in the studio commissary, where patrons —
including children — used them to wipe ketchup and grease off their
hands.

Other costumes had been badly stored and were rotting on their
hangers. Beautiful lace gowns had cobwebs, and the dust of thirty
years covered everything. When he touched some of the dresses worn
by Irene Dunne, Katherine Hepburn, and Ginger Rogers, and designed by Hollywood's best couturiers, they fell to pieces. How, he
wondered, could so much history, so many beautiful things be so
badly treated? He wanted to rescue these things.

Berman's didn't collect the RKO wardrobe immediately. Kent
and his colleagues would go over and pull costumes when they were
needed, but it was obvious that much of the wardrobe was too old to
be used or saved. The salvage job was put off until the last minute,
when Desilu wanted the storage areas cleared. Finally, Berman's
decided to throw most of it away.

In a rush, Kent went to the studio and loaded up his trunk. He
found a lot of good wardrobe, costumes with big star names, which
nobody knew or cared were there. Berman's knew what Kent was
doing and he was told he could take whatever he wanted. But there
wasn't enough time to get everything.

From *Top Hat*, he found Ginger Rogers' riding suit, with plaid
coat and beige pants. He also located her heavily beaded, fur-lined
dress from *Follow the Fleet*. He found bow ties, a wonderful pair of
slippers and a vintage white tuxedo worn by Astaire in one movie, the
right size for Kent. This was the beginning of Kent's personal costume collection.

* * *

At Berman's, Kent was known as a flamboyant fellow. He loved
old cars and had a Model A Ford, which he often drove home for

lunch. One of his favorite gags was to go over to Ladies Wardrobe and pick out the biggest, wildest woman's hat he could find, stick it on his head and rush down Santa Monica Boulevard, feathers flying, from Kings Road to his home on Stanley Avenue. He did it for laughs, more than anything; that was his style.

But he was also brash in serious ways. His talent blossomed while he worked at Berman's, so much so that he recognized that he was worth far more than his grim wage. He had the ability to turn rags into beautiful costumes and a knack for finding the most difficult things. One day, he surprised co-workers by walking into Mr. Berman's office and demanding a raise, and not just for himself, but for another costumer as well. "I'm leaving if we don't get paid $125 a week!" he told the boss. He got the raise. But that wasn't all he got from Berman's. He also got a reputation for having light fingers.

Kent lived at 1422 Stanley with another costumer, Ron Wind. Ron was taller than Kent, had dark brown hair combed flat against his head, and oily skin, but a fair complexion. He fell into work at CBS Television City in the mid-1960s and stayed there for many years. He would do anything for Kent, and together the two men were quite a pair.

Their house was a run down affair built in the 1940s, with little of the charm left that was once native to Los Angeles. Thelma White, the star of the famed *Reefer Madness* and leader of the All Girl Band, lived in the house behind theirs. She raised bald Japanese chickens and was a frequent visitor to Ron and Kent's.

Their house was filled with joy. The two men brightened their home with parties and laughter that carried well into many nights. They both had energy to spend and burn. They were "hot" all over town, and to them the world was a place to be conquered.

Kent especially was mad for decorating; he turned every loose dime into furniture and art from the past, chiefly Art Nouveau and Art Deco. Through the front door visitors walked into another land, a land that only Hollywood could understand. Movie collectibles were everywhere, re-creating an atmosphere that never really existed, except in the minds of the occupants.

The decorating and parties required only one link to reality: money. And money was Kent's and Ron's game. They understood money, made it, played with it, then got some more. For a couple of young men living off the bare threads of their profession, they always had cash to spend. And friends didn't ask questions.

* * *

The mid-1960s was a golden time for acquiring Hollywood memorabilia because the old studio system was breaking down. The moguls were either dying off or already had died, and the studios were selling their back lots, sound stages, costume and prop departments to big corporations buying into the movie industry. The new stockholders didn't know anything about movie-making, much less Hollywood's history, they were just interested in the bottom line.

Some of the studios were being sold to television — like RKO to Desilu — and with these sales came huge packages of movies, including all the studio key books on individual films, press books with publicity photos, biographies and clippings, and various script drafts. The new owners rarely wanted little more than a couple of stills to announce the TV package of films and so all the rest of this stuff was up for grabs.

It was a golden time, if you had a truck and unrestricted access to the studios. It was a perfect time for Kent and Ron and they went into action.

Ron was the first to find value in these abandoned treasures. Whenever possible, he "liberated" stills — publicity photographs, movie frames and such — from the hands of those at the studio who would have thrown them away. At some of the book stores along Hollywood Boulevard, like Collector's Book Store, which opened in 1965 and dealt exclusively in movie material, Ron could sell his stills for a quarter, fifty cents or a dollar a pop. Ron collected studio stills like a madman, then sold them to this new market of fans and dealers who were willing to pay good cash.

It didn't take Ron long to figure out that there were more valuable relics from Hollywood's past that had been forgotten and might be thrown away. He looked toward "liberating" props and costumes and to do this enlisted the help of Kent.

Ron Wind got a reputation for taking anything that wasn't nailed down, and even then, he'd get a crowbar. When it came to rummaging, he was like a spiderman; he could get up into any area, especially the rafters of old sound stages, where studio personnel often had stashed props and costumes. But Ron really didn't know what he was looking for. Kent had the eye of a connoisseur, and told Ron what to get.

A neighbor remembered Kent and Ron because of a Tiffany lamp that had hung in their dining room, and the story that went with it. One of the young men had discovered it hanging, thick with dust, on a stage at Paramount. In the middle of an ordinary day on the lot, Ron climbed the catwalks and loosened the lamp from its hook, then scampered down and outside to Kent's jazzy jalopy. They stuffed the booty into the trunk and quickly motored out the front gate. In such a hurry to get away, they didn't realize that the lamp's chain was dangling, kicking up sparks as they tore down Melrose. The story of the dangling chain came up often and kept the men laughing.

There were other stories, about dropping clothes out of windows at Western Costume, or loading the trunk, in broad daylight, at every major studio. Kent and Ron, costumers, had carte blanche to get wherever they wanted, to take what they wanted. Nobody cared, even those who knew.

Kent had the connoisseur's eye, and first pick of whatever he and Ron happened to get. Ron just wanted to sell the stuff, getting rid of it quickly. He sold gowns to thrift stores for a few dollars, if nobody else was interested. Kent wanted to keep certain things, which is where the two men differed.

Kent really cared about the costumes, especially the fine cloaks and gowns that summoned memories of his childhood fantasies. He cared most for the clothes that were from the best movies. Ginger Rogers' dresses were wonderful, not because they were so beautiful, which they also were, but because she had worn them. Having the dresses in his hands connected Kent directly with the past. He wanted to perfect his own image of the past. He placed emotional and sentimental value far above the material level that Ron worshipped. Kent was not the stealing sort. He would never take from a person; quite the contrary, he wanted to give.

* * *

Ron and Kent had a small picture in the living room, a photo that was taken on April 5, 1965, of the two of them with Judy Garland; documented proof of Kent's passionate fondness for the tragic star, which helped explain why the ruby slippers were so important to him.

The photo had been taken at the Governor's Ball, following the 37th Academy Awards ceremony. How Kent and Ron got the tickets to the annual gala, I didn't know, but a friend who worked with Kent at Berman's remembered being green with envy. Kent had been in Hollywood less than a year, and here he was going to the industry's premiere event.

The night belonged to Julie Andrews, who won the Oscar for Best Actress in Mary Poppins. Andrews thanked Jack Warner in her victory speech, because he had turned her down that year for the part of Eliza in My Fair Lady, a role she had created for the stage.

In contrast to Andrews' happiness that evening, an ominous, tear-filled cloud loomed over the ceremony. Judy Garland was supposed to sing. It was like waiting for a train wreck, and the anticipation and tension filled the Santa Monica Civic Auditorium. The Awards were being broadcast to millions of homes on live television. People crossed their fingers, some whispered silent prayers. Would Judy make it?

The program called for Judy to perform a medley of Cole Porter hits, a tribute to the composer who had died the year before. Roger Edens, a lifelong friend, had arranged the number for Judy. She was scared, said Garland historian John Fricke. She was wound up in absolute knots. Everybody was pulling for her, saying, 'C'mon, Judy, you can do it.' And she did. For those in the audience, her moment was exhilarating. She had the rare power to make people feel good, despite her personal tragedies.

Kent and Ron, both immaculately dressed in tuxedos, must have been overwhelmed to be near her, their Hollywood star, their desperate queen on top of the mountain of belief, the holder of their dreams, in maybe her final flash of warming light — they wanted to be near her more than life itself. To be near her at the Governor's Ball turned out to be quite easy.

The traditional post-ceremony party was held that year in the Grand Ballroom of the Beverly Hilton Hotel on Wilshire Boulevard. By the time Kent and Ron arrived, Judy was already sitting at a center table, flanked by two talking men, waving hands and cigarettes. She clutched the stem of a champagne glass with her fingertips. Her eyes stared at nothing, on a straight line to the middle of nowhere, but the boys could see the lost laugh of a child and a thousand tears.

Kent and Ron found that they could pass behind her table with ease. They could practically touch her, even say hello, but she didn't seem to notice. She didn't care. To be near her was easy, but they wanted a picture.

They hailed a photographer, a Hollywood paparazzo named Jack Schnitzer. Carefully, the boys knelt down behind Judy, while Schnitzer took the photo from the front of the table. It looked as though Kent and Ron were seated next to her, but they were mugging for the camera, peeking over Judy's head. They kept it framed in the living room.

* * *

Kent was not the stealing sort. He would never take from a person; quite the contrary, he wanted to give. Kent understood the clothes to represent something much greater than money; they were God-given, man-made treasures that deserved to be preserved. But when he found himself immersed in the upheaval that was Hollywood in the 1960s, he became a modern-day prince in a Mach-iavellian wardrobe world. He was in the right place at the right time. But fortune, as the Italian philosopher explained, rules only half our actions; only those who act upon fortune prevail. Kent acted.

Very rationally, within a year of his arrival in the costuming industry, he had sized up the immediate situation. The studios were "trashing" important history. It had to be saved. He believed this in his heart, which was fortified every time he touched some fabulous costume that he specifically remembered from a movie. He would be filled with the energy of the scene, an energy he couldn't explain. He couldn't understand why people didn't want these things. Just throw them away? No. He'd take them. Rescue them. Save them. "Liberate" them.

Sometimes he took costumes that were already in the dumpsters, which he regularly checked, but only when he had learned that some costumes had been thrown away. In 1966, he worked at Warner Brothers on the production of *Camelot*. It was a big-budget musical, and most other studio needs were subordinate to those of this movie. Consequently, Kent had the run of the lot.

His job on *Camelot* was that of a "second" costumer, or costumer's assistant. His talents proved invaluable. He was given the task of dying many costumes to achieve colors that best presented the medieval time frame of the movie. His work was brilliant and he was credited by his superiors for creating the beautiful costume colors on screen.

John Truscott, the designer of *Camelot*, was so pleased with Kent's work that he gave him one of his costume sketches; later Kent would boast of having received from Truscott the envelope which announced that the 1967 Academy Award for costume design was John Truscott, for *Camelot*.

But *Camelot* was not Kent's most involving work at Warner Brothers. While he was there, he learned that a significant portion of the Warner costume collection was being systematically and matter-of-factly destroyed. Bins of old clothes were regularly sent to the incinerators. Kent made a practice of going through the bins at night. Among other things, he found a tan-colored London Fog trench coat that looked very familiar. The inside label read: "Humphrey Bogart." It was from *Casablanca*. And it was "liberated."

* * *

The very nature of Kent's work took him to all the studio wardrobe departments and all the costume houses. He got to know the wardrobe people, even the gate guards. He could drive his car anywhere on any lot, carrying a duffel bag, or an armful of costumes. Clothes were always being pulled for current projects, taken to the cleaners, or rented and returned.

He quickly learned that costumes were spread all over town, that a coat worn by Robert Taylor in an MGM film might be found at Fox, or at Western Costume. This occurred through a studio practice known as "counting hangers." For fifty years before Kent had arrived in Hollywood, the studios had been swapping costumes, and these costumes borrowed between studios were accounted by the number of hangers, not by the star or the tailor.

When RKO filmed *Fort Apache* in 1947, they put out a call to all the studio wardrobe departments for cowboy and Indian costumes, along with a number of U. S. Army Cavalry suits. RKO bought some costumes outright; others were rented from MGM and Western Costume. For the production, each costume was specifically tagged, but when the film finished shooting, each costume was not specifically returned.

If RKO had rented 30 Cavalry costumes from MGM, then costumers counted 30 hangers of Cavalry costumes and they were returned to MGM. Rarely were the 30 costumes exactly the same as those that had been borrowed or rented. That's why it was not unusual for Kent to find clothes at Berman's worn by Marilyn Monroe in movies she had made at Fox.

At first, Kent thought the system, or lack thereof, confusing, because it made hunting for specific costumes all the more difficult. They weren't always where he thought they'd be. But the searching catch-as-catch-can only helped him to lift clothes. Nobody kept specific, star-related inventories. Nobody noticed when specific pieces, no matter how prominent, disappeared. The studio wardrobe industry operated on the honor system. Kent honored the system in his own way, because he honestly believed he was saving costumes from destruction. And he was.

Soon Kent mastered various tricks of the trade. Beneath a large hoop dress, for example, there was enough room to underhang other costumes without detection. In this fashion, Kent could legitimately rent one costume and walk out with four.

* * *

There was no diabolical plan, no conspiracy or method to Kent's liberating ways; it was simply "look what I brought home today." He and Ron got wild about costume "liberty."

Word-of-mouth around town was that everywhere, costumes were being thrown away. People began to scramble, wanting to get the wardrobe out of studio hands to put the more important pieces into caring hands. Ron was happy grabbing handfuls of anything; Kent realized there wasn't enough time to be everywhere, so he searched only for the best. Often, Ron and Kent disagreed on how to dispose of so many costumes, once they were liberated.

Ron just wanted to sell, sell, sell. Kent thought of the costumes as breeders regard puppies; he wanted to find good homes for the pieces, to put them into the hands of collectors, where they would be appreciated. Both men developed lists of buyers. Ron found clothing shops and second-hand stores that would pay him a dollar or two per piece; and Kent found collectors crazy about Greta Garbo, Marilyn Monroe, Rudolph Valentino, Humphrey Bogart, Lauren Bacall, Leslie Caron, Gene Tierney, Robert Taylor, and virtually every other major star of the Golden Era.

Transactions were made with little noise and almost always in cash, although Kent had no problem with selling on time. But he always kept the costume until the final payment. Kent sold much less in volume than Ron, but he sold the best pieces. When it came to Hollywood memorabilia, he had a sense of style that his prices reflected. "You're buying memories," he reminded collectors, "not just threads."

Kent's convenient stories covered his tracks, if buyers asked about provenance. He'd gotten the item at a garage sale, or a used clothing store, he would say, which was plausible. Second-hand joints often purchased studio clothing at discount rates. Kent was a regular at these places, usually when he was working. If he found something he liked, he'd buy it for five dollars, or more often, he would trade.

In this fashion, Kent collected everything. He bargained and bartered at every opportunity. He was an expert, the consummate wheeler-dealer. He believed in the worth of nostalgia, to the point where he often traded it as a commodity on a real futures market that existed on the streets. And he always traded up, acquiring better and better pieces. Hollywood memorabilia became his calling.

* * *

"IF I ONLY HAD A BRAIN"

I had hoped that a call to the Costumers Union Local 705 would reveal Kent Warner's work history. While records of current members were closed to public scrutiny, those of the deceased should be available.

Bill Howard answered my call. He had been the business representative for the Local for 25 years, and handled most of the intimate questions directed to the union. A no-nonsense man, he gave me what I asked for.

"Work records are up to the individual," Howard said. Kent had tended his well, listing employment from the mid-sixties until his death.

Howard read from Kent's card: "Warner Brothers, 1966; Desilu, MGM, 1967; Desilu, CBS, 1968; CBS, Paramount, MGM, 1969; MGM, 1970; MGM, Warner Brothers, 1971 and 1972; Universal, 1975; Universal, Orion, 1976; Universal, from 1977 until 1981; then Stephen J. Cannell."

Kent didn't join the Local until 1972, but that obviously hadn't prevented him from working on almost every studio lot during his first seven years in the business. "He was a good costumer," Howard told me, "a hard worker."

I asked Howard what he thought about Kent's taking the ruby slippers. That kind of activity, he said, was certainly not common in the industry but, "then again, I don't know of a costumer who hasn't taken something."

I knew what he meant. Costumers enjoyed "perks" of their trade. He didn't mean costumers were crooks; I thought he was defending Kent.

* * *

A costumer at Universal gave me the names of two men who might have worked with Kent. The first was Bill Jobe. He told me he had worked with Kent for a short time at Universal, but hadn't known him very well. They were colleagues on the lot, he said, but not friends at home.

The second name was Carl Garrison. "So much has been said about the red shoes," he said. "I heard there were six pairs made. One original pair I saw at the MGM auction. They were sold, and Sammy Davis, Jr. has them."

"Judy Garland was asked if she wanted a pair," Garrison continued without changing his breath, "but she said 'no,' and I don't believe she took a pair. What did she want with her movie wardrobe?

"There was a pair stolen… " he trailed. "The person who bought the shoes at the auction lodged a complaint, saying they were not the real slippers. Any one of six pairs could be real but… The person who showed them to me stole them." The person was Kent Warner, he said.

I asked if Garrison had seen a pair of ruby slippers?

"Yes," he said. "I asked Kent if he had a bill of sale. He said 'possession is nine-tenths of the law.' Kent was a little, mincing blond, with a moustache. He was boastful about everything. Very flamboyant, no remorse. When I asked him 'aren't you worried someone will say you stole the slippers,' he said 'let them prove it.' That's what I remember about Kent.

"In the business, a lot of wardrobe people feel old clothes are up for grabs. Rather than let it lie there and rot, they took things home. Kent happened to be in a prime position to clean things out. I'm sure he had an idea of their worth. He said, 'I bought them. Let 'em prove that I stole them.'

"I assumed that he sold his pair to Sammy Davis for $25,000," Garrison concluded.

* * *

A call to Sammy Davis, Jr. netted fool's gold. His publicist, using the modern miracle of conference calling put me directly on line with a cheerful Mrs. Davis, who excitedly said, "Yes, we have the ruby slippers. They were a gift from Liza." I believed her.

Next I rang New York, but Liza Minnelli's people were much less cooperative. "She is not available, can I take a message?" I left the question: "Did Liza give Sammy Davis, Jr. the ruby slippers?" A week later the answer came back, by way of relayed message: "Yes."

I felt a bit elated. I had uncovered one pair of the slippers, or so it seemed. Not until months later did I learn that slipper sightings could be deceiving.

While I was speaking with Jack Haley, he said that he, Liza, and Lorna Luft all had been given replicas of the ruby slippers in 1976. It was the Ruby Slipper Award, given by a charitable foundation. They had been the first recipients. "Liza didn't have the real thing," Haley said. So neither did Sammy. Ka-blooey.

* * *

Kent's last Hollywood credit was as Wardrobe Department Supervisor for Stephen J. Cannell Productions. He built the department, starting as its only costumer and working out of a closet at NBC Studios in Burbank. Cannell, the prolific writer and producer of episodic television who gained fame for *Rockford Files,* had built a small empire in a short period and Kent was part of the family. Sheila Mason, who succeeded him in that position, said she had memories of Kent, both good and bad. "I went through so much with him. It was dreadful watching him turn into an old man."

At her office in Culver City, where Cannell's wardrobe department had grown with hit after network hit into a building of its own, the handsome woman said, "This is my place. We moved in just a few years ago. Kent never worked here."

Sheila said that she and Kent had first become acquainted at Universal years before, when both were assigned to a movie called *Swashbuckler*. For three months they were shooting on location in Mexico. They had worked very hard on the project but still managed to have quite a bit of fun together and developed a close friendship. Kent admired Sheila because of her willingness to put in long hours and the fact that she never said "no" to a producer's wardrobe request, no matter how difficult or ridiculous.

Working with Cannell kept Kent extremely busy. The producer had received network commitments for two new programs when Kent joined the company — *Quest* and *Greatest American Hero* — and Kent was the designer on both. As the sole designer for the company then, he got to build every costume from scratch. At 39, he was entering the prime of his profession. It was clear to everyone who worked with the highly charged young man that his best work was yet to come. Nothing seemed likely to stop him.

But even Kent could not keep up with Cannell's success without help. As the company expanded, so did the wardrobe department; Kent was told he could add a costumer. He hired Sheila.

"Kent joined Cannell in 1979 or 1980," she said, "and brought me over in 1981. We had worked together at Universal, well, not together, we did different shows, but we saw a lot of one another. He had an office there, which was filled with old radios and memorabilia. He had a big collection. Marilyn Monroe, televisions, Ginger Rogers, though I didn't know he had the ruby slippers. What I remember is that he had a marvelous collection of research books, exquisite books. After he died, his family sold everything. High prices, to pay doctor's bills I guess, although I think he sold the radio collection intact.

"He was so talented," she said, "and such a perfectionist that he couldn't tolerate anything less, and he got on people if their work didn't match his expectations. He was difficult to work with that way. But then again, he would help you find anything.

"I know Kent was very private and guarded his personal life. He kept it separate from work. We didn't talk much about love interests, though I know someone broke his heart, hurt him deeply toward the end." She paused on the thought, wondering if she should tell me more.

"Kent thought Connie Sellica was the most beautiful woman on Earth. He loved her beauty. During *Greatest American Hero*, he could hardly stand to be in the same room with her, he was that over-whelmed by her. I remember he designed a dress for her, not something for the program, but for a dinner party. He really took care of her. He really was wonderful. I miss him."

Sheila's deepest memories of Kent brought tears. "I watched him die for three years, and he worked right up until the end. I got in-volved, or tried... "

She leaned back in the chair behind her desk, surveying her station with a gaze that said "Kent should be sitting here." The job was his. Then she picked up a black address book that was lying on top of some papers. "I don't know why I kept this," she said. "It belonged to Kent."

***

"IF I ONLY HAD A HEART"

Chronicling Kent's life proved to be no easy task. From his interview with the *Los Angeles Times* I learned a little about his childhood, and from Sheila Mason of the few years before his death. But I needed to fill in between 1964 and 1980 — the years he flourished. Then, out of the blue, I received a call from a young man whose first words were "I dated Kent." We agreed to meet at his home in the Hollywood Hills.

Trent Taylor thinks he met Kent at a cocktail party, about the time Kent went to work for Edith Head at Universal. Head was in her dotage so Kent did most of the designing, which was a dream come true, but it also frustrated him. It took Trent a while to understand why.

Trent remembers sharing "six intense months" of his life with Kent. He remembers Kent's platinum blond hair, blue eyes, "handsome face and puppy dog smile." These are the qualities that attracted Trent to Kent.

"I have four rules for dating," Trent said. "The person must be able to read, must be able to write, have a car and a job. When I met Kent, he didn't have a car. What a shame, I thought. How can I go out with this man, no matter how charming he is? He said it was in the shop.

"Well, he did have a car, a beautiful beige-and-white Corvette, 1956. It took weeks to come out of the shop, but when it did, he said 'I'm going to take you out for a date,' and he did.

"He took me to a candlelight dinner and he just charmed me, but he drove like a maniac, like someone in a hurry to his funeral. He would drink, then drive with horrible abandon, like a taxi driver in India. He'd get behind the wheel after four drinks, talk madly about Ginger Rogers and run a red light. He was very self-destructive, an accident waiting to happen. He didn't have car insurance because it was too expensive. He had a couple of accidents, but he never said anything. That didn't fit his image.

"Kent was a very visual person. He probably stood out in school because he had trouble writing. I once saw a note he wrote to his maid. It was something. I think he was dyslexic. But dyslexic people, you know, they're usually very creative.

"He probably spent a lot of time alone, and maybe had the best times of his life when he was alone, like the time he spent in that attic that belonged to a friend of his grandmother's. He found all those beautiful clothes. They must have really turned him on, not sexually. But just to touch them and visualize them on people. Imagine how he felt when he found all these famous gowns from Hollywood.

"Kent was 32 going on 14, when I met him. He looked young. He was working on a movie called *FM* at Universal. He sparkled. This guy was just flashing electricity. Absolutely adorable.

"He was very focused on his career and his collecting. His radio and television collection was invaluable. If it had stayed intact, it would have gone to a museum. He loved the design of the tubes in the cases. Old televisions were high Deco to Kent. Here was a box with so much going on inside. He loved the creation.

"He had all the televisions in one room, at least most of them. It was a small apartment, but it was beautifully furnished with his collections. He had radios and microphones—I asked him about all of them because I knew what they were and could hold intelligent conversations about them, but I didn't say a word about the slippers.

"They were prominently displayed in the apartment, but I pretended they weren't there. They were on a square pedestal, about four-and-a-half feet tall, and were covered with a Lucite™ box, with a little plastic stand to elevate them. At first I couldn't figure out what they were, so I didn't mention them. I was there six times before he finally asked, 'Aren't you going to say anything about my ruby slippers?'

"He took them out of the case and showed me the bottoms. He showed me where Judy tapped her heels together. They had little, circular scuff marks. He said they were worn only in that scene. I almost fainted. He knew he had the best.

"His finding the ruby slippers was like seeing the light. They were a real prize to him, which he treasured, just like the TVs. They transcended costume, they were art, just like most everything in his collection. He had an appreciation of value for things.

"The MGM auction was his stamp of approval with his peers, and he got to go through all these wonderful Hollywood things from the movies he remembered and loved most. I don't know what he did with all his costumes. I never saw him sell a thing. He was a gentleman when it came to business. If somebody called when I was there, I never knew it; he'd say he'd have to call them later. He ran all his business that way; he took those calls alone.

"Many people wanted things from him, but people rarely had anything he wanted. A lot of people disliked him out of jealousy and lack of knowledge. I guess that's what happened with a lot of the collecting, especially with the costumes. But he always had a lot of cash — maybe too much cash.

"He was a compulsive buyer. He couldn't keep money in his pocket, whether he was spoiling himself or someone else. But the things he'd buy, he had a developed, studied taste, the kind you can't teach. Kent had style. And funny!

"Kent could make the checker at the grocery store smile for three hours after he left — he had that kind of infectious sense of humor. He could take different abstract ideas and put them together into something funny. He was not spiritual, he was right here and now, wired to a 12-volt battery, wired to live.

"After Kent and I had been together for a while, a girlfriend of mine invited me to Hawaii. I told Kent that I would be gone for a week and that I'd see him when I got back. He didn't say anything, but I guess he felt terrible.

"I didn't send him any postcards or call. He and his mother spoke on the phone almost every day, I imagine. He was used to that kind of relationship. I broke his heart, people said.

"I didn't see him for a little while after I got back, then we ran into each other at a cocktail party. I saw him alone in the kitchen.

"I was wearing a beautiful pair of white linen pants, I'll never forget. They cost $150, and he knew what they were — it was his business. While we were standing there talking, he destroyed my pants with his drink. All over the front of them. He was terribly sorry and offered to pay for a new pair, or to have them cleaned. Like a gentleman, I politely refused and stayed at the party. It was an accident, or so it seemed then. Looking back, it couldn't have been anything but a subconscious move to get even.

"A few weeks later I saw him at another party. He was with a vacuous, 22-year-old street kid with tattoos. They were both falling over drunk. I worried they would have an accident. By the standards of the day, he was not promiscuous.

"Three or four years later, about 1981, I ran into him at a market, right in the parking lot. I never shopped there and neither did he; we were both sent there for a reason. It was the only time he expressed his feelings to me and told me what an impact I'd had on him. He was sincere, he really meant what he was saying.

"I suppose if I'd called him up and we'd gone out to dinner, he would have never said those things. It was the spontaneity of the moment. He had that kind of honesty. But he was very destructive to himself, especially with his drinking.

"Kent had beautiful eyes, but there was more going on behind them than you could see. He had one of those timeless faces, and the kind of body that looked good without going to the gym. He was slender, but well put together, and prone to intense relationships. He liked to run the show, be the star of every circle. It was hard for him to find people on his level.

"He was very close to his mother, they were connected at the hip. She adored him. I met her once and she was beautiful, a lovely woman, very well met. No one could ever have loved him as much as she did. She was probably blind to his sexuality because of it, and he could never be completely honest with her. He never wanted to be anything less than perfect.

"He had trouble writing and he couldn't draw. Imagine a costume designer, oozing with talent, who couldn't draw? Adrian was his idol, and he loved designing. Kent had that kind of talent but couldn't express it.

"One of the problems with Kent was that he was so visually oriented that the visual image was more important to him than the reality. When reality overrode image, it was really shocking to him. He had to be rid of it. That was all part of denial, like he denied having AIDS. What a terrible waste."

* * *

THE HAUNTED FOREST

Sheila Mason opened Kent's black address book, folding back page after page. "His writing was poor," she said. "You can see that." The book was filled with business numbers and addresses. The first entries were neatly written. "He had one of the secretaries write them in," Sheila remembered. The additions were in Kent's hand, which looked like fourth grade printing. Touching the book somehow fortified her enough to tell me about his last days.

Late in 1981, a time when Cannell was extremely busy, Kent came down with a bad sore throat, which persisted, off and on, through the New Year. He was never one to be sick; he didn't have time. The hyper-energy of his life had always kept him healthy and at work, and work couldn't have been any better. Typically, he ignored the malady.

Soon, the condition worsened. Kent hated doctors, but finally went to get checked. His bad throat caused him continual colds and infected his tonsils. How stupid, he must have thought. He didn't want a child's ailment to put him in a hospital bed. But the doctor said he needed surgery: a tonsillectomy.

Kent made the arrangements, requesting time off and making sure Sheila would be able to handle the burden of costuming two network shows. Then, the morning he was supposed to undergo surgery, he called Sheila from home.

"I'm not going into the hospital," he said, "but I'm going to take the day off." His sore throat and tonsils felt much better. Kent came back to work the next day. But the condition persisted.

* * *

Through 1982, Kent continued to get colds and have a sore throat. He said the doctors had determined it was not his tonsils, but an ulcer on his esophagus. He had trouble swallowing food, and drank gallons of ulcer medicine. He kept a quart-sized white bottle on his desk and gulped from it frequently. But the medicine soothed only the symptom; soon he started to lose weight.

Sometimes he would snap at Sheila, or other Cannell employees.

"He ran hot and cold," Sheila said. "He could be mean to people, or the sweetest man. Now I know it had to do with his illness, but I didn't know then."

Kent's once vibrant, high cheeks sagged into sallow holes in the middle of his face. His muscles disappeared. In a matter of months, he became an old man. He couldn't keep food in his body, which further depleted his flesh of badly needed nutrients. He had his worst pain going to the bathroom, but nobody ever mentioned AIDS. Medical science had just discovered the virus and the public was ignorant. *Time* and *Newsweek* were still covering herpes.

By the Spring of 1983, Kent was a very sick man. Sheila urged him to go home for a while, to go to the doctor, to the hospital, and get well. Kent refused the advice for several months, but he quietly tied up loose ends.

He found buyers for many of his possessions. He needed money to pay the medical bills and to secure a down payment for his own condominium, which he purchased in Studio City that year. He also sold his old Corvette and, uncharacteristically, bought a new Mercedes. Kent never drove new cars; he always had old classics. This was a bold departure for him.

At work, things also began to change. With the addition of *The A-Team* and two other shows to Cannell's production schedule, the department was acquiring more and more full-time personnel and needed a titular department head. Kent was in line for the position, but because of his illness, the call went first to Sheila.

She persisted in begging Kent to take a break, go home and get some real rest. He finally relented because his body was clearly failing him. Some people whispered that Sheila wanted Kent out of the picture so that she would get the job as new department head. Kent knew better. Before Sheila accepted, she called Kent and told him what was going on. For Sheila, it was an impossible situation. She didn't even want the administrative position. She was happy costuming. She wanted to know if Kent would be back soon because, if so, the job should be his. She asked his opinion.

There really was no choice; Sheila became the department head. That Christmas, she visited Kent and hugged him. He felt like a bag of skin and bones. But he said he was coming back. The company, in its family-oriented wisdom, had offered Kent a department head's title if and when he was ready to return to work, and even put the title on his *A-Team* credit. He decided to honor their offer and for a few months in 1984, he returned to his daily pattern of going to work at the Cannell wardrobe office at NBC.

By then, the little man had no energy. He could barely work a couple of hours a day, so Sheila constantly covered for him. If a director called and wanted this or that, Sheila would say Kent was in the bathroom, or at lunch, or on a run to the cleaners. She used up every possible excuse; still, everybody knew it was because Kent was sick.

One night in February of 1984, Sheila was at home watching a television documentary about a young man who was being drummed out of the military because he had AIDS. Though the man's face was masked, Sheila could swear she was listening to Kent. The story of their separate fights against illness was the same. Sheila learned of the killer disease: Acquired Immune Deficiency Syndrome. There could be no more frightening words to her that Spring.

* * *

Easter came late that year, on April 22. For the first time that anyone could remember, the Costumer's Union had declared Good Friday a studio holiday. Kent didn't believe it.

The subject came up on Maundy Thursday. Kent had come into the office but didn't have the strength to do anything. He was in pain,

Sheila said. The pants he wore — a pair of designer jeans with an immaculate crease down the front — were hurting him because the front button was putting pressure on his backbone. His stomach had fully deteriorated.

"Why don't you go home, Kent," Sheila said. "You can rest up during the long weekend." Kent didn't understand, and she explained that Good Friday was a holiday. He had her call the union to double check, right in front of him. When he knew it was true, he asked Sheila if she would walk him to his car. She said yes and, as they walked, she held his hand.

"He had trouble finding his car," Sheila said. Kent hadn't told her he was going blind. "We walked all around the NBC studio parking lot, until he finally found it." He was driving an old Ford, or Chevy, she remembered. "What happened to the Mercedes?" she asked him. "I sold it. Too much trouble," he said.

Kent offered to drive Sheila back to the front gate of the studio, since they had walked so far, and as she sat in the car next to him, she asked him what was wrong. "You should go to the hospital and get well," she urged him.

"Someday, we'll sit down and have a long talk and I'll tell you the whole story," he said. Sheila nearly cried; she hugged him, as much as she could hold of what was left of the frail man. "That was the last time I saw him."

* * *

On Easter, Kent entered the UCLA Medical Center suffering from septic shock and peritonitis. He died three days later, on Wednesday April 25, 1984, at 5:40 in the afternoon. He was forty-one years old.

While the world watched Ronald Reagan on his historic trip to China, and the Kennedys mourned the drug overdose of RFK's young David, a warm Santa Ana wind covered the Los Angeles basin, whipping temperatures up into the 90s, carrying the energy of Kent's soul to the heavens.

There was no announcement in any of the Hollywood trades. Only the Costumer's Union newsletter would print any notification, and long after Kent had been buried.

Services at Forest Lawn in the Hollywood Hills were private, attended by Kent's family and only a few of his closest friends. Kent's mother had decided he should be buried there. His life was in Hollywood, and that's where his memory should remain.

It was an unusual service in that words were not spoken. Words were not good enough to describe Kent. On a beautiful Saturday in Southern California—the type of day Kent liked to spend at flea markets—the mourners stood in silence on the hillside, while the casket was lowered into the ground. They watched in silence while friends and family took a hand at pouring shovel after shovel full of dirt onto the casket, silence while the spade packed the last handful of earth on a mound of memories.

* * *

A PAIR OF LOUSY SHOES

There is no measure to gauge the depth of a mother's grief, and I was a fool to think more about ruby slippers than the greater human question.

Kent's mother had sold all of his collected possessions after his death — his televisions, costumes, books, furniture, everything except the most private mementos. I knew that Kent had sold one pair of ruby slippers at auction, but did he leave a second pair to his family? Leo, the costumer at MGM's wardrobe department, mentioned it. "Kent might have willed a pair to his family, to his mother and sister." I wanted to find his mother and ask.

The Costumer's Union had a number listed on Kent's card, but it had been disconnected. I found no new listing, and put the thought on the back burner.

One afternoon, in the Spring of 1987, a Texan rang my phone.

"I am the representative of a wealthy man who would like to purchase a pair of the ruby slippers. I understand you may know of a pair for sale." ·

"How'd you get my number?" I asked.

"From a man at MGM, in the wardrobe department. He said you knew where the slippers are."

That wasn't entirely correct. I knew where some of the slippers were. There was the Smithsonian pair, safely ensconced; there were Roberta Bauman's slippers, tucked inside a shoe box at her Memphis home; there was the pair that Kent Warner had sold at Christie's in 1981. That's all I knew for certain. But I supposed there were more. As for any pairs for sale, I couldn't say.

"Money is not a problem," the Texan said. But turning this smooth-talking voice onto Roberta Bauman didn't seem right. "Can you help us find a pair of the shoes?"

"Maybe," I said, as I stared at a slice of Southern California sunshine cutting across the wall of my room. "But I'm not in the business of buying and selling ruby slippers. I'm no broker. I'm interested in information."

"What do you want to know?"

"There's a woman who might be holding a pair of the slippers, might be willing to sell." I was talking about Kent Warner's mother. Perhaps this fellow could help me find her.

"What's the problem? She wants to sell, we want to buy."

"I've never spoken to her," I said. "I don't have her number or address."

"What's her name?" asked the Texan. I wasn't ready to tell him but I did anyway and regretted it as soon as the words drooled off my tongue.

"Have you tried directory assistance on her?" he asked. "Yes. There's an old number listed. Out of service." I guessed she had moved.

"Well," he drawled, "we got a few friends here and there and might be able to get a reverse directory check on her. What city did she live in?" I told him that, too. "And her old number, do you remember?"

"Just a minute," I said. "I'll look it up."

I reached for the phone book, a new one. I hadn't looked up the name in months. There was a new number. The frog in my stomach jumped.

"I can't find it," I lied. But the Texan heard my change of tone well enough to say, "Thanks a bunch for the help," and he hung up. Within a couple of minutes, Kent Warner's unsuspecting mother answered her telephone. The Texan got to her first.

* * *

"That was quite a conversation," the Texan said when he called me back. "She was listed in the phone book." I felt like a duck in a swimming pool.

"She got a little angry when I asked about the slippers."

I cringed. "What did she say?"

"She said she didn't have a pair, but then her husband—I guess it was her husband—gets on the line and says '$40,000, put up or shut up,' and she takes the phone back and says not to listen to the old man. 'He's sick,' she says, and then she says again that she doesn't have a pair of the slippers. But I don't know? Why would the old guy say anything if she didn't have the shoes?"

The Texan's question made me wonder, too. But questions about ruby slippers echoed the hollow din of a tin bell against the resounding tragedy of a mother's loss. I needed to talk to Kent's mother, for my own petty curiosity, but what about her? Did she need to talk to me? I wanted to be sensitive. I dialed her number.

* * *

"There isn't anything at all I know about my son's business," Kent's mother said with the strength and grace of a noble woman bothered by a fly around the eye. "All I cared about was whether he was eating and going to the bathroom. That's the honest truth."

Sadly, she could not erase Kent's association with the ruby slippers—he must inexorably be connected with them—but her focus sharpened on the triviality of my search: "I do not own a pair of ruby slippers; I do not own a pair and I really don't care. If you knew how little they meant to certain people. Why would anybody be involved with a pair of shoes, a pair of lousy shoes that belong to a person that did a movie? How absolutely unimportant."

The Texan had done me no favors. Kent's mother refused to talk about her son. Within this mighty little story I began to find simultaneous attraction and repulsion to every thought about the ruby slippers.

* * *

Through newspaper articles I learned that only months after Kent
Warner's passing, the ruby slipper trail twisted up through San Francisco. On Tuesday afternoon, October 16, 1984, San Francisco police
had been called to a novelty store at 1467 Pine Street. The owner said
he'd been robbed. The officers learned that a pair of Judy Garland's
ruby slippers had been taken at gunpoint by thieves. The owner
valued the slippers at $20,000. The SFPD immediately recognized
this was an odd case.

The store itself was odd. Called Humpty Dumpty & Sons, it was
situated on Pine near Polk Street, just west of Nob Hill. It had not
been open long, and featured a wide and weird variety of fantasy
paraphernalia that the owner said he had collected for the better part
of 20 years. The owner was a bit of a personality in the city, a real
clown.

Twice in the past three years, he had been featured in local newspaper articles. The most recent had appeared in the *San Francisco
Examiner* just a couple of months before the robbery. About-town
columnist Stephanie Salter had given his place a great plug. "There
are novelty stores and magic shops and stores full of kitsch," she
wrote. "Then there is Humpty Dumpty & Sons, the realized dream
of a gentle soul named Ted Smith."

Salter profiled Smith as "the child of circus performers... who
also once worked as an organ grinder with a monkey." He was known
around San Francisco as "Raggedy Robin," a professional clown with
a penchant for buying memorabilia. "I'm like a little kid with a big

shopping bag," Smith said. "For years I would buy stashes of things. People were always saying, 'So, where's the shop?' "

The reporter detailed the contents of Smith's store, calling it a place that "can keep a bored child or adult delighted for hours." Smith had "filled the store with inexpensive, irresistible playthings," she wrote, along with an "impressive collection of antique toys and artwork."

"Basically, I buy things that I like," Smith told Salter. "Some of them aren't for sale. This is a museum as well as a shop. I want this place to be a kind of therapy, where people can come in and get away from how hard it is in the city. I'm doing a kind of magic in here. It's a way for people to get renewed."

Among Smith's collections were a mechanical chimpanzee in a bellman's uniform, lobster claw harmonicas and kaleidoscopes. There was memorabilia from Playland-at-the-Sea and "giant canvas sideshow banners from the heyday of Ringling Brothers."

He had a teddy bear display, which Salter explained brought back memories of "the bear he lost as a child in a flood. It was the same bear his brother once had put in the oven." And he had "turn-of-the-century ventriloquist's dummies, carved wooden dolls and merry-go-round lions.

"There are T-shirts," Salter added, "including one Smith dreamed up: a drawing of Joan Crawford, who insists, 'I never touched the bitch!' And there are racks of eclectic cards, ranging from overt gay sexpots to Maxfield Parrish prints."

More than anything else, Smith's store celebrated *The Wizard of Oz*. Smith advertised the store with a flyer that featured Billie Burke as Glinda the Good Witch, holding her magic wand. "Come out, come out wherever you are to the Greatest Little Shop this side of Munchkinland!" read the copy. Smith beckoned patrons to come visit "A Magical Emporium, A Palace of Wonders, a Phantasmagoria of Whimsical Delights to Gladden Your Heart."

"Visit our Happy Hall of Hilarity," he wrote, and "see Dorothy's Ruby Slippers." Smith had a picture of the shoes inset at the bottom.

Shoppers visiting the store couldn't miss Smith's devotion to *The Wizard of Oz*. There, enshrined in a corner, were effigies of the fabled Yellow Brick Four. Locked in a separate glass case, Smith kept the ruby slippers.

"I think *The Wizard of Oz* had a tremendous effect on Americans," Smith told Salter. "It was a psychodrama. Everything that happens in the movie, you can believe emotionally."

* * *

Salter's article, though, was not the first place Smith had announced that he owned a pair of the ruby slippers. Two years before, *San Francisco Chronicle* reporter Randy Shilts (who went on to write the most comprehensive and telling book on the AIDS epidemic), had written about Smith and his pair of ruby slippers. Shilts wrote that Smith was selling his pair. "A Sign of Hard Times," the headline said. "Oz Ruby Slippers Must Go."

In the article, published April 13, 1982, Smith recounted his childhood desire to own Dorothy's magical shoes. "I knew I wanted those slippers a lot more than the Wicked Witch did," Smith told Shilts.

Smith gushed about the slippers, telling Shilts how important they were. "*The Wizard of Oz* was an American Iliad," Smith said. "It means to me what the Bible or Koran might mean to other people."

"Despite the religious fervor Smith lavishes on the red pumps," Shilts wrote, "the collector has decided to sell what he says is one of the ten pairs of ruby slippers made for Judy Garland." Shilts cited Smith's T-shirt business, noting the success of his Joan Crawford "Mommie Dearest" line; the reporter explained that Smith needed money to bring out a new series of T-shirts featuring Nancy Reagan ("Let Them Eat Ketchup") and *The Wizard of Oz*.

Shilts didn't say what Smith was asking, but said, "If the past is any indication, the innocuous, stage-glittered shoes with slick red soles might pull a hefty price," and he recounted sales figures from the MGM and Christie's auctions.

Shilts described the slippers as a pair of size 6, 1930s-style pumps covered with red sequins and a rhinestoned-bow, sitting on a satin pillow in Smith's living room. He wisely added that "verification of Smith's booty... is a sticky issue," and reported that Smith said "he bought his pair from a former MGM costume department employee some eight years ago."

"The authentication is seeing them," Smith said. He told Shilts that he expected them to sell. "Things like this do well in a depressed time because people are nostalgic for the better times, times that were so much more innocent than now."

But apparently, the shoes did not do well enough, because there they were, waiting for the thieves who entered Humpty Dumpty & Sons two years later. The thieves came at 1:30 in the afternoon.

* * *

Smith told police that "two men came into his novelty store, pulled a gun and demanded that he place the size 6 shoes worn by Judy Garland... in an empty cardboard box."

"Of all the things for them to take," he whined. Smith declined to say what he had paid for them but estimated their value at $20,000. He told reporters that he had purchased them ten years before from a man who worked at the MGM wardrobe department. Smith described the shoes as "red-sequined, leather-lined, bowed slippers with the label, 'Innes Shoe Co. Hollywood-Pasadena-Los Angeles.'" He said he was offering $10,000 for their return.

Newspaper reporters had a field day with the story as they playfully wrote headlines and copy. "Oh Toto!" said one. "Dorothy may never get back to Kansas." Another kidded; "Oz Slippers in Wicked Hands." An Associated Press wire story said "two gunmen — instead of one wicked witch — made off with a pair of ruby slippers."

Smith was quoted as saying that the robbers "must be on the Wicked Witch's side. I hope somebody clicks the heels three times and the slippers come back home," he said. "I feel like something very important has fallen into insensitive hands."

As armed robberies went, it was a story that everybody in the country could identify with, including Roberta Bauman in Memphis. Once again, she couldn't believe what she was reading. She was familiar with Ted Smith.

As the years had gone by, the intensity of Roberta's local celebrity had worn off, but the cards kept coming, and every now and then she'd get a phone call from someone who wanted to know more about her ruby slippers. Roberta always obliged, with detailed information, hoping the inquirers got what they wanted.

On December 29, 1981, Roberta got a phone call from a man named Ted Smith, who said, as she recorded in notes of the conversation, that he was a free-lance writer in San Francisco who wanted to write a story about her ruby slippers. Roberta said she would be happy to provide him with whatever information he wanted.

Soon after, Roberta sat down and wrote Smith a letter, "telling him all about my pair of Judy Garland ruby slippers." Roberta copied down all the information she had, told her story, copied her newspaper clippings, took photos and mailed everything "in a nice envelope, first class."

Roberta did not hear anything back from Smith until March 6, 1982, when she received a letter from him.

> "I am sorry that I have not been able to write you earlier. Since the last time I spoke to you on the phone, I have been in Boston. My father was killed in an auto accident a few days after I spoke to you and I have been in Boston helping my mother. It was a hard experience for both of us. I convinced my mother to come out and live here with me, which she'll be doing in a few months time.
>
> "But now it's back to work for me and picking up where I left off on my ruby slippers article. One thing happened while I was away that may account for why I haven't received anything from you. The Post Office

here somehow lost a lot of the mail that they were holding for me. I regret to say that I suspect your letters
were probably among that lot. I am hoping that you will
be able to still send me some photos and information
about the ruby slippers that I requested before. I am
enclosing $5 for your expense of film. I need a good
close-up photo, a side view, and photos of the bottom.
What color is the felt on the bottom of the shoes... "

Roberta thought these were peculiar requests from someone
writing about the ruby slippers—would he publish all the photographs, she wondered? She read on:

"Please see if you can take a close-up of the shoes
from the front. What color is the inside of the shoe?
What were the numbers on the inside and where do
they appear? What are the size and dimensions of the
shoes?"

Smith closed his letter by thanking Roberta and writing, "I will
send you a copy of the article after it is published." He wished her "a
beautiful day," and signed his letter, including a return address on
Fillmore Street in San Francisco.

Roberta was so moved by Smith's sincerity that she sent him,
again, all the information he had requested, along with photos from
all views.

* * *

Just as Dorothy's ruby slippers took her down the Yellow Brick
Road to meet the Scarecrow, Tin Woodman and Cowardly Lion,
Roberta's ruby slippers introduced her to new friends. For her, 1982
was a big year, which brought her into contact with Tod Machin and
another Oz fan, Barry Barsamian, who lived in Oakland, California.
Both Tod and Barry asked Roberta many questions, and she mailed

them photos and information, similar to that which she had prepared for Ted Smith. Both Tod and Barry became part of her network of ruby slipper friends.

Roberta, out of her own generosity, informed Tod of Ted Smith, "the writer in San Francisco." Maybe Tod would like to write Ted, too, she reckoned. Tod did.

Not long after, Roberta received an unusual package in the mail from Barry Barsamian. It contained a newspaper clipping from the *San Francisco Chronicle* about the ruby slippers. It was Randy Shilt's interview with Ted Smith. Roberta couldn't believe what she was reading.

"I'll have to cry all the way to the bank," Smith told Shilts in the interview. "Just to think that Judy Garland touched these is amazing." Amazing is what Roberta thought of Ted Smith.

* * *

On May 2, shortly after reading the *San Francisco Chronicle* article about Smith, Roberta sat down and wrote a letter to Tod.

> "... I am apologizing for giving you the name of Ted Smith after what I learned about that person. Here he talked to me 30 minutes from San Francisco and also talked to you. Did he at any time reveal he owned a pair of the ruby slippers? He did not mention them to me.
>
> "I was honest, truthful, sincere... and to have him give me the line he was a free-lance writer and wrote for the *New York Times* and etc. No telling what kinda line this turkey is feeding others. Well I assure you, I will write him off ..."

Tod was not ready to do that. He was embroiled in ruby slipper research for his college term paper. If Smith really did have a pair, Tod wanted information from him. But because of Roberta, Tod was very skeptical. His first move was to write the *San Francisco Chronicle* and ask for a copy of the photograph that had accompanied Shilts's article. "It was all set up," Tod said. "They were going to have it made and send it to me. Then Ted called and I happened to mention the photo to him. Several weeks later the paper called and said they were sorry that the photograph could not be made available to me."

The next time they talked, Tod told Smith that he didn't think Smith's shoes were used in the movie.

"Why do you think that?" Smith asked.

"For one," Tod said, "there's no Innes label, and two, the center stone in the bow of your shoes is round, and the ones in the movie are square." Smith asked Tod how he had gotten hold of the *Chronicle* photo? Tod said he hadn't.

* * *

After he graduated from college in 1984, Tod visited Ted Smith's shop, Humpty Dumpty & Sons. He could look for himself and decide if Smith had an authentic pair of the ruby slippers.

"It was an impressive store," Tod said. "He had huge, wonderful things. All around the ceiling were these enormous plaster clown heads, enormous clown faces with big grinning teeth leering down at me. It was a little scary. On the wall, he had a big picture of the Wicked Witch going after the shoes. He had some wonderful collectibles, some very expensive things, but he didn't have a real pair of the ruby slippers."

Smith was not in the store when Tod walked in, but Tod left a message at the desk and later the two men met. Tod confronted him with the stories Smith told Roberta. Smith admitted that not all of what he had said and done was true. He admitted conning Roberta to get information, Tod said. "He felt bad, but he thought that was the only way she'd help him."

"The bottom line with Ted Smith is that he wanted a pair of the slippers, and if he couldn't have a real pair, he wanted a pair that looked closely like them. His pair were not up to snuff. They were hideous," Tod said.

When Tod reported to Roberta, she felt vindicated. "I'm glad he got Ted Smith to admit his lie about the ruby slippers," she wrote in her notes. "Some gag! I wonder if the SF newspapers found out it was a stunt."

If the San Francisco papers didn't find out that Smith had pulled a stunt, at least the San Francisco Police Department concluded that he had. "It was our belief that he concocted the whole story," said Inspector Frank Harrington, who handled the case. "We were never able to verify that he actually owned a real pair. We believe they were fakes. The case is closed as far as we're concerned."

* * *

During several odd phone conversations, Smith told me he did own a pair of the ruby slippers. "I bought them from somebody at MGM many years ago. They were a bargain. They came to me from a second source. Word was they were taken from MGM prior to the auction. I always believed these were possibly Judy's shoes." When I asked about the theft, Smith said "It was a very bad incident. I was widely known for collecting things at the time. I was pretty well known. There was insurance on the shop, but I never filed a claim. I did file a police report. It's a dead issue now, it's closed."

Then Smith waxed on about the shoes: "They do have a power, but you have to deal with it. I wore them very well, but they weren't rightfully mine. They really are the Witch's shoes. I have their essence. I stole them, I destroyed them. Maybe I poured all my troubles into them, and they represent all my hopes and fears. I borrowed those shoes to become a part of me. I don't think I abused them. They're not that important. I think I'm a little like the man who wrote the book; I'm not a very factual person. I do delight in the mystery of it."

* * *

The "mystery of it," as Smith mused, turned out to be a huge fabrication, which I verified through Jack Townsend, the ruby slipper replica maker. Smith read Townsend's advertisement in the collector's magazine and immediately wrote to him. Townsend forwarded me a copy of the letter, dated March 3, 1982:

> Dear Jack:
>   Your phone call was the hi-point of the day. It is so seldom that I get to enjoy the company of someone who is intense about *Oz* as I am... I hope we can meet someday.
>   Enclosed is $250 plus for Blue Label UPS $4. Please send off the Ruby Slippers ASAP. I am full of appreciation & I will always treasure them and regard you as a friend. You can visit me whenever you come to San Francisco.
>   I hope you don't think I'm the Wicked Witch of the West asking for all your goodies — right now I have this enormous feeling for you in my heart...
>   Best wishes for a bright day,
>   Ted

When I confronted Smith with this information, he could only admit that he had lied to Roberta Bauman.

In one way, the alleged slipper robbery represented a symbolic way to close a chapter in Ted Smith's life. Within days after he reported the slippers stolen, Humpty Dumpty & Sons went belly up.

* * *

The entire San Francisco slipper story seemed a terrible diversion, wasting so much time and energy on a fruitless search for a pair of shoes that didn't exist, but a happenstance thread, no doubt ruby red, connected everything together.

At my request a friend of mine in San Francisco stopped by 1467 Pine Street to tell me what Smith's old store looked like. Once there, he met a man named Don Ritchie, the proprietor of an antique store now at that address. Ritchie had inherited the shop when Smith went bankrupt.

Ritchie didn't claim to be an expert on the ruby slippers, but he did speak from some experience when he said that Smith's pair — which he'd seen — did not look like the real thing. How did he know? "I had a friend from the old days who had a pair of the ruby slippers in his living room," he told me. The friend's name was Kent Warner.

* * *

"BUT THAT'S FUNNY... I'M SURE WE'VE MET SOMEWHERE BEFORE"

Don Ritchie had known Kent from the "old days." They had met, not in San Francisco, but in Pasadena, at a Rose Bowl swap meet. That Ritchie took over Ted Smith's store was an eerie coincidence which enabled me to "meet" Kent Warner through the memories of surviving friends. I wondered about the "charm" of the slippers.

The "old days" had begun in 1971, when Kent went shopping at the Rose Bowl swap meet — one of Kent's favorite haunts — and stopped by the stall operated by Ritchie and his friend Ken Maley. The two young San Franciscans, collectors of antiques and Americana, frequently "swapped" at the Bowl, which meant regular trips between the Bay Area and Los Angeles. Maley also owned a small retail business on Melrose Avenue that he tended on his Southern California trips.

Kent had stopped at their space to look at a lighter that Maley was selling. Kent, Maley remembered, "liked smoking paraphernalia." It was not that he was searching for pipes or bongs, like the youth of the 60s; Kent had a passion for strike-tip lighters, the primary smoking accouterment of the 1930s. He didn't even smoke cigarettes. He just liked the look and feel of old lighters. Holding one in his palm, feeling the weight inside the smooth, metal skin, looking at the shine and the Deco design, made him feel good. In the "old days," Kent always carried a lighter in his pocket to proudly use when a friend had a smoke.

Maley remembered talking with the attractive young man for some time and exchanging phone numbers. It wasn't long before Maley and Ritchie fell into company with Kent and his roommate,

David. The four men became close friends and spent weekends together.

Sometimes Kent and David went to San Francisco. The first time they stayed in a motel, but after that they "moved in" with Maley and Ritchie. Kent was high-strung and always worried about his weight, "but he was a head-turner," said Maley.

Kent loved the scene that was San Francisco in the 1970s and mixed freely with the open lifestyle that existed there long before it came to West Hollywood. But he was not comfortable with the entire scene because of his mother.

"Kent had a piece of sheet music framed on the wall," said Ritchie. *The Shadow, He Knows*, was the title, but someone had carefully inked in an 'S', *"The Shadow, She Knows."* Maley didn't know where the nickname came from, but he gathered it was old from a story Kent had told.

It had something to do with when Kent lived with his mother and would go out prowling and not return until the dark hours of the morning. One time, he swore, he saw a shadow on the wall. It was his mother. She always knew where he was and what he was up to. They were that close. "The Shadow," Maley sighed. "She was a mysterious figure to me. I got the feeling she was more than middle class. Kind of wild."

Ritchie saw the framed sheet music in the Hollywood home on Highland Avenue that Kent and David shared. When Ritchie and Maley visited Southern California, they stayed there. Both men were quite impressed with the magnitude and quality of Kent's collecting.

They couldn't help but notice the ruby slippers. Kent kept them on display in the corner of his living room, on a four-foot pedestal, covered with a plexiglass hood and with a spotlight shining directly down on them. The sequins sparkled just right. They were the focal point of all reverence in the room. Maley said he thought the slippers had been sold at the MGM auction. Kent just laughed. He'd tell them that story later.

* * *

Ritchie and Maley remembered specific things about Kent and David's home. In the foyer was a white statue that Kent said was from the 1939 MGM movie, *The Women*. It was highly stylized Art Deco, a woman cast in a seductive pose with the right arm raised over her hair. The statue was life size, at least six feet tall.

The decor matched the period of the statue. Porcelain figurines made of rare German glass, lighters, radios, clocks and armoires, all things from the recent past. It was like walking into a post-war home in the 1940s. There was no worry.

Kent had a cabinet full of precious movie memorabilia, including Fred Astaire's shoes and bow ties. There were costumes everywhere, on hangers, in boxes, on display. Even more costumes were in the closet where Ritchie and Maley stowed their weekend gear.

One costume, in particular, neither Ritchie nor Maley could forget. It was a silver, fur-lined, bugle-bead gown, lavishly displayed on a mannequin near the living room. Neither Ritchie nor Maley knew immediately how important the dress was to Kent, and to Hollywood history, until they saw it later in a movie.

* * *

Kent's idea of a good party was to invite a few friends over to watch movies. Before the dawn of the video cassette, this was a big home event. Kent had his own 16mm projector and a library of films. He especially liked to show movies for which he had costumes and props.

He liked to put the projector outside and aim it through a closed window onto a projection screen in the living room. That way, Kent told friends, it was more like being in a movie theater. Also, Kent didn't like the noise of the projector.

Rogers and Astaire films were popular with Kent. One night, while Maley and Ritchie visited, Kent showed one of his favorites, *Follow the Fleet*. Toward the end of the movie, he stopped the projector, then walked into another room. In a few minutes, Kent returned wearing the beaded silver gown. It had been worn by Ginger Rogers while she danced with Fred Astaire in the film's climactic scene.

Kent was no drag queen; he was reliving the scene in his living room, imitating Rogers by slapping at the air with the long, fur-trimmed sleeve. Kent acted among friends to make the men laugh and show off the gown, not for any other reason. The friends marveled at how easily Kent had acquired these important mementos of movie dreams. The Ginger Rogers dress was just one of many items in Kent's vast wardrobe collection that Maley called "the first stop" between the studios and the streets.

There were Norma Shearer dresses, uniforms from *Star Trek*, Bogart suits, lavish cocktail gowns worn by Leslie Caron and swash-buckler outfits belonging to Errol Flynn; all would find buyers eager to possess such wardrobe for a hundred dollars here, fifty bucks there.

Kent appreciated costumes as film history, Maley said. It was just good timing that allowed him to make money by saving these things.

* * *

Kent was a sexy little man, very aggressive, and had a thing for money. Among his closer friends was a collector of antiques and Deco pieces named Paul Tiberio. Tiberio owned a store on Robertson Boulevard, where Beverly Hills meets West Hollywood. Actress Jane Withers was one of his frequent customers.

Paul and Kent were of the same ilk and they profited handsome-ly together. Paul's store featured many Deco pieces right out of Hollywood's 1930s. Paul and Kent worked together.

"They loved to torture each other," Maley remembered. "Paul was outrageously expensive for the time. Not many collectors could afford his pieces. If he got a piece that he knew Kent would want, he'd call and they'd haggle over the price. They tortured each other that way. They loved it."

Besides using the films in his library for entertainment, Kent watched them for costumes and props. "He would look through the films and stop them," Maley said, "study them and then go out and find the objects." He kept lists of costumes he was looking for, especially for particular buyers. Then Maley shocked me: "He had a standing list of things Debbie Reynolds wanted. She was one of his first customers. There weren't a lot of people involved."

* * *

"Kent always complained that Debbie Reynolds was cheap," Maley said. "She always wanted Kent to give her something for free. She wanted people to give her memorabilia for free, for the museum. Kent made a point of selling everything, he wasn't risking his neck for free. But because she knew the studio system and what was going on, she was able to deal with Kent in a fashion he understood. They both got what they wanted.

"Kent had a relationship with Debbie," Maley said. "They were very close. She knew he was taking stuff. She was one of his best customers. She knew where it was coming from. She always got the best price because she knew. And she was buying like crazy.

"Debbie was an instant source of money for Kent," Maley remembered. "She had an obsession. She would meet him in parking lots, places like Thrifty's on Sunset. Afterwards we would always celebrate with a bottle of Dom Perignon."

* * *

Ken Maley was not the first person to mention Paul Tiberio's name to me. Leo at MGM had said he was one of Kent's best friends, had been at the funeral, and bought many of his possessions.

"Kent's mother held the garage sale of all time after he died," Leo said. "Only a few people knew, and Paul Tiberio was one of them. I didn't find out soon enough, but I heard about it. Even though the prices were high, Kent's things were the best."

Trent Taylor also knew Tiberio through Kent. "Mr. Deco," he called him. "He drove a Rolls Royce and sold things to Barbara Streisand. His prices were always too expensive."

I would have liked to talk with Tiberio about Kent, but his life had become part of the larger tragedy. I learned that he had died in February, 1987.

* * *

KENT'S SECRETS

Kent and his roommate David lived together for several years in the early 1970s, during the time Kent enjoyed his notoriety as "The Keeper of the Shoes." I found David listed in the phone directory, after Ken Maley gave me his name.

"The real story of the ruby slippers, and the one that must be observed," David told me, "is that one pair were sold at auction, and one pair only."

David obviously knew. "Life has taken strange turns in the past couple of years," he lamented, while giving careful thought to whether he should talk with me. "Some information was given in confidence, even it if was almost 20 years ago. I always had great admiration for Kent. I'll have to think and check with a few friends to find out if it's time to talk about Kent."

Time to talk came several weeks later. "I have talked with a few of the people around at that time, who were interested and intrigued. Kent's gone now," David said, "and why not? He was for the preservation of Hollywood." So we began.

"It's not that easy to describe Kent. Outgoing, but that may have been only a persona for presentation. He was a very intense human being, unusual, all wrapped up in a tight little ball. Kent was a bouncing-off-the-wall type person, high energy, highly motivated, especially toward his work."

David told me that much of Kent's energy had been absorbed by his passion for collecting, especially memorable items that once belonged to his favorite movie stars or to his favorite movie designer, Adrian. "Kent loved anything by Adrian," David said. "He idolized

Adrian. From the MGM auction, he even got a couple of sketches signed by Adrian. He kept one of them on the refrigerator.

"Kent was a real collector. He liked old cars, old radios, old televisions. He had a collection of 78 recordings. I used to drive his MG. He had a beautiful 1949 MG TC that he let me drive to school. He also had a 1938 Oldsmobile Business Coupe, an old Corvette and a beautiful old Mercedes.

"I know that at one point, maybe Kent was out of work. I remember calling him from Hawaii, in 1980 or 1981, and he told me he was thinking of selling the slippers. He was trying to target the MGM Grand Hotel. It seemed to me he thought of it then, but he did tell me he was going to sell them. I asked him how he could part with them. He said some things were no longer important to him.

"As Kent realized his illness, he gave things to friends. I don't know what happened to everything, but before he passed away, he wondered if people who own these things might sit on them. He did not want that to happen."

Why Kent chose to sell his prized pair of ruby slippers no one knew. They apparently had become more of a distraction than an attraction in his life. This surprised friends.

For such a long time, the slippers had meant so much to Kent. They were much more than just a piece of Hollywood memorabilia, much more than a valuable piece of industry history. They transcended Hollywood, to the point where they represented the powerful image of innocence to all America.

Kent understood the importance of the slippers and so he sought them when he realized that they were within his grasp. He would find them and save them from destruction, restore them, clean them, prepare them for show. He poured the energy of his soul into them and he was proud of them. They brought him influence, power and respect among friends. And they did this because he believed in their magic, in their charm, which he shared with everyone who asked about the slippers.

The charm of the slippers plainly wore Kent out. Rather than energize him, they sapped his energy. More and more, people wanted to know about the slippers, and not about Kent. Their draw was magical, but overpowering to the point where Kent could no longer bear witness to his own stories about the slippers. He first grew bored; beyond bored. The shoes became a source of pure ennui. It was as if he had vanquished their charm and was left with nothing but the burden.

People who visited Kent's home and saw the slippers wanted to talk about them. Didn't anyone want to talk about anything else? It got to the point where he packed them up and put them in a closet. They had worn him out.

How long Kent thought about selling the slippers isn't known, but he first put them up for auction in December, 1980. The slippers, and a gingham dress Kent owned, were the feature items offered by Wizard Productions in what was billed as a Movie Memorabilia auction.

Charles Band of Los Angeles was the auction's promoter but remembered little about Kent. "The shoes were offered very quietly," Band remembered, implying that Kent didn't want anyone to know his identity. "And he wanted a lot of money, more than anyone bid. He kept the shoes."

For the auction, which was held at the Ambassador Hotel, Kent estimated a going price of $20,000 to $75,000. He would not sell them for anything less than the lower figure but hoped they would bring much more. They didn't, which left Kent disbelieving. He knew they were worth much more than $75,000; they were priceless. Didn't anyone appreciate their value besides him?

By the end of the auction, Kent was angry. He heard all the snickering about the shoes from people he considered a bunch of third-rate poster dealers. These people didn't know memorabilia. "They just wanted to spend a nickel on a poster that's worth a dime," he said to a friend. "A bunch of cheapskates. I'll show them."

Immediately after the Christmas holidays, Kent contacted Christie's East in New York. Kent was determined to show that an established auction house would bring a proper price for his ruby slippers. Christie's demanded a low reserve, which Kent reluctantly accepted. But he felt good about the auction, in part because he was dealing with Julie Collier. She was very excited about the slippers.

In 1981, collectors of Hollywood memorabilia were still very confused about the nature of the business. Nobody knew how many pairs of ruby slippers existed, nor much more about them. They were a mystery. The pair Kent offered at Christie's were the third to publicly surface. How many more were there? people wondered. And what were they worth? Still, Kent believed the market would tell the real value of the ruby slippers.

When the gavel came down at $12,000, Kent sighed. It was a lot of money, but not what he dreamed. So quite simply, he sold his treasured ruby slippers. If nothing else, Kent learned that the power of the slippers was not good forever; and if it was abused, their power was wicked.

* * *

By finding David, I couldn't help but feel I'd tapped into the source of the truth. "I knew all of Kent's secrets," he had said. Urgently and obtrusively, I asked crude, naive questions about the ruby slippers: How many had Kent found? How many had he kept? "I understand Kent found seven pairs," David said. "He said he destroyed three.

"Kent loved to tell stories, and facts seem kind of illusive, especially with friends. The story became dogma over the years. Kent said he found seven pairs. Some were in boxes, some in brown paper. Apparently, there was an old costumer assisting him. The shoes were in a very dim, dark place, in a big bin, maybe down at one end, and kind of tucked away. Up high, he said. Three pairs were in very sad repair.

"Kent had the nicest pair. They were absolutely pristine. They did not have orange felt on them. They had a soft leather sole and there was no wear. He kept the ones he felt were in the best condition. I always said they belonged to the Wicked Witch of the East.

"I cleaned them; there was no damage to the sequins. Nothing inside. They were on a white, Lucite™ pedestal, covered with plexiglass, and lighted from below. The spotlight I installed myself. But I don't remember seeing Judy's name.

"He was a very devoted fan of Ginger Rogers and Judy Garland. Kent knew everything about them. He said Judy was a size 5, but wore a 6 when she danced. He examined all the shoes before deciding what to do.

"He also found the test shoes. I saw the test shoes. They were designed in red, in an exotic Arabian style, turned up in the toes and more jeweled. Debbie Reynolds has them. Kent said he was told by the auctioneers to destroy all but one pair, and he had to have a witness, he said. Someone who would tell the auctioneers he had destroyed them. I guess that was part of the mystery."

"What," I asked, "did Kent do with the remaining shoes?"

"One pair went for a quiet payoff to the witness." "Who was that?" I asked. David couldn't be sure, but he guessed it had been the old costumer. "It was a big secret, he never said."

"One pair went to the auction. They were not in good condition." By now I'd heard many people say the shoes in the auction were not among the best. This gave credence to Richard Carroll's claim that David Weisz knew of only one pair. If he knew of any others, why would he settle for a frumpy pair?

"And, one pair went to someone else named Michael. He was a dancer or actor, I think. Kent said he gave the ruby slippers to Michael because Michael was going to give them to Debbie Reynolds for the museum. Kent wanted a good pair to go to the museum, where they would be appreciated. Debbie never got them. Michael was not one of Kent's favorite people. They did not remain friends."

* * *

David had offered three clues: the Old Costumer, someone named Michael, and Debbie Reynolds. I tried to call the actress, who was listed with several unions as reachable through her publicist, Richard Gordon.

"Debbie has spent at least one million dollars purchasing movie memorabilia," he said. "She's bought furniture, paintings, lamps, costumes — it's been her dream to open up a museum. She has enough furniture to build a huge mansion, but I don't think she has a pair of ruby slippers."

When I asked to talk with Reynolds, Gordon said to call Margie Duncan, her personal assistant, at the Debbie Reynolds Rehearsal Studio in North Hollywood. Margie, I soon realized, was very protective of Reynolds.

"Kent Warner," Margie hummed, after I had brought up his name. "Debbie met him at the auction. I think he worked for the auctioneer. She used to buy things from Kent from time to time."

"Did he offer or sell Reynolds a pair of ruby slippers?" I asked.

"That's all scuttlebutt," Duncan said. "It was all very hush-hush. I used to run into Kent from time to time. I always thought the shoes Kent had were the real McCoy."

Margie said she would relay my interview request to Debbie, but for weeks the actress never responded. The weeks turned to months and she still did not call back. As Julie Collier from Christie's had said, people were very secretive about the slippers, which only made me more inquisitive. For now, I could only follow David's other leads — the old costumer and someone named Michael.

* * *

Someone named Michael. A dancer, or an actor, but David didn't remember his last name. I turned to my ruby slipper guru, Tod Machin, who thought he knew. "Michael Shaw," said Tod. "He's the one with the shopping mall shoes."

* * *

"IF I ONLY HAD THE NERVE"

Tod Machin's unusual curiosity about the ruby slippers took him to Wichita, Kansas, in 1981, to see a pair of the shoes.

"Aside from the fact that the shoes were the most indelible movie image I'd ever been presented with," Tod said, "some friends of mine and I were working on a small newspaper called *Toto Too*. It was a paper we created about life in Kansas, a tongue-in-cheek, homespun paper. For one reason or another, we were putting on a contest and we decided to offer a pair of ruby slippers as a prize. I had to come up with a pair. What did they look like? How were they designed? I became more involved with the question and that's how the interest began. It became an obsession.

"One of my friends who worked with me on the newspaper and knew of my interest in the design of the shoes called me up one day and told me about a promotion he had heard on the radio: A pair of ruby slippers were being exhibited at a shopping mall in Wichita. I had to go. This was one of the single most important things that was happening to me. I was 20 years old.

"I took a bus down from Kansas City, a southbound Greyhound. It took about five hours. We had to detour to every podunk town to pick up passengers. In one of those towns there was this great wheat field with a wheat thrasher in the middle of it, just like on Dorothy's farm. Seeing that set the tone.

"I began imagining what it was going to be like seeing the shoes. I had envisioned going to the mall and seeing a line stretching around it with people waiting to see the ruby slippers. I thought they would be in an armed case and you'd file through, ushered by guards to keep moving, like people are ushered by the Declaration of Independence and Constitution in Washington, D.C. This was something everybody wanted to see. I thought I was going to be just another person shoved through the line. That's what was building up in my mind as I was passing through the Kansas farmlands.

"I met my friend at the mall, but it hadn't opened yet. We stood on the balcony above and looked in. It's a very contemporary mall, the Town East Mall, Wichita's biggest. As we were standing there on the balcony, I could see the shoes down in the courtyard and my heart just about dropped thirty feet.

"The reason that my heart dropped was that it was nothing like I envisioned it would be. None of these people had the respect for the shoes that I believed they warranted. It was obvious that the shoes were more important to me than anybody else.

"Well, the line was long, and people did come to see them, but what I expected in my mind wasn't there. It was a drastic difference. I told my friend how disappointed I was, but I'm the overly sensitive one in our crowd.

"We went down and waited to file through to see the shoes. They had some bleachers set up across from the display, with the shoes in view, so we sat there for several hours and watched people look at the shoes. And when there was nobody in line we went to look at the shoes for ourselves.

"Before I focused in on the shoes, I focused on how everything was displayed and how the display didn't do any justice. The costumes were propped on card tables and the slippers were sitting in a scratched and fingerprinted plexiglass box, just an arm's length away. The way this was put together, I thought that people didn't appreciate what they were. They might as well have come out of a Wheaties box.

"Then it hit me that the shoes were not red. They were a wine color, to the point of being brown. The third thing I noticed was that they were made of sequins. Sequins! That was just too conventional. That's something you go down to the dime store and get. I was expecting something not reproducible.

"Seeing this took it from being Kansas history and made it Hollywood history. As far as I was concerned, the story of *The Wizard of Oz* was the story of an actual girl from Kansas. When I saw the ruby slippers sitting there, I realized they were intended only as a motion picture prop and the rest of it was an image just tucked into my head.

"I took a long time to put everything into perspective. We talked about the shoes, about the fact that they were brown and made of sequins, but then I started really looking at the shoes, trying to focus in on the construction and realizing that this was something reproducible. I started to appreciate them for what they were.

"After seeing the shoes, I became extremely excited about costuming in general. When I went back to school, I enrolled in a costuming class. Other people did pantaloons and things. I did *Oz* costumes. That's when I realized they were a lot more complex, that they really were things of beauty.

"To the guy who owned the shoes, it was obvious that there were two people just gazing at the shoes and, because they were his pride and joy, he initiated a conversation with us. He asked me what I thought of the shoes. I told him of my initial disappointment. He was terribly offended, to the point where I didn't know if he was going to forgive me. That reinforced all the feelings I had before — that nobody understood the feelings I had for the slippers. It amazed me that he could not understand.

"The conversation went from tense to cordial. I tried to explain my point of view but he couldn't get past the fact that I was disappointed in the shoes. I tried to present my case and said it was really a great compliment. That's how much the shoes meant to me. He told us his name, and that he worked at Universal Studios in Hollywood, but he didn't say anything about where he got the slippers. It didn't matter much to me. By that time I was crazed.

"On the way to Wichita I was daydreaming in the Kansas wheat fields," Tod said, "and on the way back I was plotting to make my own pair of ruby slippers."

* * *

Michael Shaw, as Tod had said, worked at Universal Studios as a tour guide. I had a friend who worked there, and he got Shaw's number for me.

I called Shaw and told him I was writing about the ruby slippers. Did he have a pair?

"Yes," he said. "I have a pair."

He told me that he had been traveling with them during the past month. He had just put them on summer exhibit at the Sands Hotel in Atlantic City and hand-carried them there. "Hollywood on Tour," he told me. "I've also got Judy's dress from *The Wizard of Oz.*"

During the seven years since Ted saw Shaw's slippers in Wichita and the time of my call, Shaw had travelled his pair to more than 25 cities where more than a million people had seen the shoes.

I asked him if he had known Kent Warner. He was surprised I knew the name. "I was told Kent sold you your pair," I said, which he didn't deny. But, suddenly he had a problem with my questions. Why did I care how many pairs Kent had found? "To me," Shaw said, "it just destroys the mystique. To go into all this folderol is offensive." I back-pedalled the conversation to my interest in the history of the film, as it related to Baum's story and the parable on populism. "Hollywood and history have collided on more important movies," he said. "I think *The Wizard of Oz* had no impact on history."

"But the shoes," I said. "People want to see them. They're desirable, they mean something."

"The purpose of your work would only disillusion and sadden people," he said. "As far as publishing, I'd never do that. It's like saying, here's the Easter Bunny— I'm going to cut his ears off. Why destroy the mystique? It's the most watched movie in the world. Three billion people have seen it. People see something in that movie that they love. That's what makes the ruby slippers the most beloved piece of movie memorabilia in the whole world. Not even the green velvet dress from *Gone With The Wind* would bring as many smiles." I didn't have to be convinced. I just wanted to ask more questions.

One week later I called Michael back. He was more relaxed and began to talk freely of his collection. "I have three of the best pieces of movie memorabilia," he said. "I have the slippers, the Maltese Falcon statue, which took four years of negotiating with a prop master to get, and I have Humphrey Bogart's trench coat from *Casablanca*." Then he opened up:

"Kent enabled me to acquire the nucleus of my collection. From what he helped me acquire, I was able to build a wonderful collection." Besides the top three, Shaw had Errol Flynn's sword from *Sea Hawk*, Margaret Hamilton's Wicked Witch hat and the grandfather clock and portrait from *Laura*.

"Kent was an unusual guy," Shaw said. "Easy to love, easy to hate. He was mad about Art Deco. He never stole from individuals, but acquired an awful lot of things from the studios." Shaw said he had been with Kent when he found Bogart's trench coat at Warner Brothers, "ready to be burned."

"When he went to work for the MGM auction, he told me, 'Michael, the main reason I went to work for Weisz was to find the ruby slippers.' He told me point blank that the only reason he went to work for the Weisz people was specifically to find *Oz* pieces. He found what he was looking for. He had every test dress plus three of the Adrian dresses. He was ecstatic. And he turned the place inside out looking for the Witch's broom." Kent never found that.

"Kent would come to the studio in the morning with a duffel bag all rolled up and leave with it stuffed. He told them it was filled with things to take to the cleaners. He took them to the cleaners all right."

* * *

Michael Shaw lived in one of those monolithic apartment buildings that all look alike in the City of Our Lady, Queen of the Angels. Once through the requisite security gate, I passed into a courtyard filled with concrete and a swimming pool.

I walked down the concrete corridor to the last apartment on the first floor, tucked back in the corner of the project. Even in daylight, the entrance to his home was dark. And darker it got.

Inside, the overwhelming color was a rich brown, the warmth of the earth.

A suit of armor stood in the hallway, near a knight's helmet. On the walls were pictures, closely bunched together — movie posters and vintage 1950s Coca-Cola trays. A "3-sheet" poster of Cecil B. DeMille's 1919 production of *Male and Female* went from floor to ceiling and a "one-sheet" poster of Mary Pickford as *M'Liss* decorated the living room, on an easel. Shaw offered me a seat on the couch. There, in the living room, a beautiful pair of ruby slippers was elegantly displayed.

"When I first saw *The Wizard of Oz* I was a child actor under contract to MGM," Michael said. "I was eleven years old. I was mesmerized, enchanted by the movie. It wasn't until the late 1950s that the movie became popular, not until its sale to CBS. The movie helped to sell a lot of color televisions when CBS said it was going to be broadcast in color.

"The shoes themselves are worthless," he said. "It's what they are and what they represent. Magic. People are so familiar with them." He fell back into his comfort zone, so I pressed again. Where had Kent found the shoes?

"Kent found all the pairs on the third floor of Ladies Character Wardrobe at MGM. All the pairs were lined up on a shoe rack, covered with dust," he said. "It was quite a climb to the third floor. Very dirty, dusty, very bad light. Naked light bulbs. It was a room not frequented much. The ladies of the wardrobe department didn't like to climb the stairs and there was no reason to go up there. Most of the stuff was from *Oz* and *Zeigfeld* and couldn't be used for other movies. There he found the test pairs and each of the production pairs.

"I'd rather not say how many pairs he found," Shaw chirped when I asked. "I don't want my pair to lose their impact." He was coy about it, but I thought he really didn't know.

"There were four pairs known to be worn by Judy Garland," he offered, as if conceding me a morsel of wisdom that I could take home with me. "And Liza never had a pair. Debbie Reynolds asked her if she wanted to purchase a pair at the auction and Liza said 'no, I don't want a pair.' "

"How do you know that?" I asked.

"Debbie and I go back many years. I worked for her for three-and-a-half years, as her curator, and then we had a big blowup."

I wondered if the blowup had to do with the ruby slippers.

"I was at the MGM auction constantly," he said. "I bought many costumes, including one from *Ben Hur*. I paid $2 for Peter Ustinov's costume in *Quo Vadis*. Thousands of people were there."

Michael said that he had sat next to Reynolds at the auction. He said that she did not even bid on the shoes, something I had already known, but now I knew why. One thing I could never understand was why a woman who was said to have spent more than $100,000 at the auction would not consider $15,000 of it for the most important piece of Hollywood movie memorabilia.

Did Debbie know that Kent had other pairs of the shoes? Michael smiled when I asked the question. I'd uncovered a Hollywood secret. Debbie was probably being a little bit catty when she told Aljean Harmetz that the shoes being auctioned were "too big for her and thus must have belonged to Garland's stand-in."

A picture of Shaw and Reynolds that day flashed through my head. Debbie, in her black and white suit, sitting on a red folding chair in a room full of red folding chairs, waiting for the big event. People milling around her, asking for her autograph, while paparazzi snapped quick pictures. And sitting near her, in his own red folding chair, was Shaw, obviously smiling with deep, knowing eyes while the world was oblivious to him and the secret that he shared with Debbie. He was a bit catty himself when he interrupted my picture.

"When the schmegegee who paid $15,000 for the ruby slippers found out they were not the only pair, he had a fit." Michael chuckled. "Right after the MGM auction, Jack Valenti contacted me about the Sakowitz department store doing a 50th anniversary display for Hollywood. They wanted to display a pair of the ruby slippers," he continued. Shaw had agreed, he said, and that resulted in the public debut of his traveling shoes. Shaw thus began to cash in on his investment.

"While the shoes are on display, Bob Sakowitz hands me a telegram from schmegegee's lawyer saying he had the only pair of ruby slippers. 'I represent the man who bought the shoes,' the wire said. I sent one back to him, quickly explaining Hollywood reality. I made the deal with Kent before the auction. I never heard back from him."

Again I pictured Michael sitting at the MGM auction in his red folding chair, next to Debbie Reynolds, the two of them smiling, knowing not to bid. It was time to pop my question.

But I didn't have the courage to ask him face to face.

* * *

Two days later I summoned the nerve to call him. "Michael," I said, "I have to ask you this question: Were you supposed to give Debbie Reynolds the pair of ruby slippers you bought from Kent?"

He exploded, instantly.

"That's absolutely false! My pair of shoes... I purchased them from Kent! I paid good money for them. I bought them, I had to borrow money. I had to give him the money in cash. He brought the shoes and the dress over himself. It's an incredible lie! I would submit to a polygraph test. That's how angry I am!"

* * *

"THESE THINGS MUST BE DONE DELICATELY"

Debbie Reynolds has long been known as dedicated to preserving Hollywood's history. For years, she has lobbied the studios and the press to establish a Hollywood museum.

In an interview while promoting her book, Debbie Reynolds chronicled her interest in movie memorabilia: "I started collecting Hollywood costumes and artifacts in 1970, when MGM had its first auction. It was very depressing to see the end of such a magical era, so I spent every dime I had.

"I bought costumes and props so I could re-create scenes from Academy Award-winning movies or very popular films... I bought furniture from *Gone With The Wind*, Greta Garbo's costumes from *Anna Karenina*, Clark Gable's trench coat and the costumes from films like *Annie Get Your Gun* and *The Philadelphia Story*...

"Twentieth Century Fox had an auction five years later, and of course I went. I was able to save costumes of Marilyn Monroe, Tyrone Power, and Errol Flynn's swashbuckler from the pirate movies. After that, Columbia had an auction, but there was very little left because the dissipation was terrible — robberies, stealing — but I did get a few things.

"I never really thought of collecting Debbie Reynolds memorabilia. I bought for the museum."

Indeed, Reynolds amassed what some collectors assume to be one of the largest collections in the world, but only she knows its extent for sure. The museum of her dreams never materialized, and the bulk of her collection has never been on view to the public. To some, this is a shame. Why would Reynolds collect so much for a museum that did not exist, even going so far as to ask people for donations?

My own attempts to talk with Reynolds were thwarted continually, but I persisted. I had to know: had she received a pair of ruby slippers from Kent?

After six months of repeated interview requests, I finally got a phone call from Debbie Reynolds. It was late on a Thursday night, well after eleven. She spoke slowly, and deliberately, her words trickling like drops of fine champagne out of a shallow glass.

*   *   *

"I don't have Kent's slippers," she said carefully, to begin the conversation. "I knew him just in passing. We met at the MGM costume auction. He had an opportunity to remove the slippers. It's just a story," she said.

But then, suddenly, she blurted, "and he had the slippers. There were five pair in total, but he didn't have five. He took two — I didn't know he had two pair, I was told he did. I know there were five pair made. We all had extra slippers. When I made musicals I always had at least three pair of everything. Certainly there would have been three or four pair of ruby slippers, quite easily.

"All our shoes at MGM were made at Western Costume by a man named Al. He used to come over and make all our shoes. We always had stand-in shoes.

"The pair they sold at the first auction weren't Judy's. I tried them on and we wore the same size, and I told them so. We both wore a 4-1/4, and I put the shoes on and they were like a size 8. I said, 'Well, these are not Judy's. They must belong to one of her stand-ins." So I didn't even bid on them. They sold to a man from Houston. They weren't hers anyway, so I didn't even raise my hand up.

"Mike Shaw called me shortly after the auction and said that through Kent Warner he could buy them for $2,500. I was out of money because I'd just spent $180,000 at the auction. Mike Shaw bought his, he bought his through Kent Warner." Then she admitted:

"I have a pair of slippers that Kent Warner gave me, with the curled-up toe."

"The Arabian slippers?" I asked.

"The Arabian slippers, they're red ruby slippers with the rolled-up toe. They were a test pair."

I was interested in the test pair, but didn't want to get into that just yet. I wanted to know her thoughts about Kent's selling Michael Shaw the pair of ruby slippers.

"I know that Kent sold them to Mike with the full belief that the museum would get them," she said.

"Was this the source of a feud?" I asked.

"I have no feud with Michael Shaw whatsoever. He and his father bought the slippers. He bought them from Kent. When he bought them he said, 'You know they're yours, Debbie, they're for the museum.' I said, 'That's wonderful, they'll make a marvelous exhibit,' and I haven't heard from him since. That was 1973 or 1974. Certainly we have no argument. I haven't talked to the man in 15 years. If we're having an argument, it certainly is a quiet one."

* * *

Maybe he and Reynolds weren't having an argument, but Michael Shaw wasn't being quiet, at least to me. "It's a lie," he declared. "Tell me, if the pair of shoes that I've got were supposed to go to Debbie, why didn't he give them to her? Debbie would have made Kent a firm money offer for something as precious as the ruby slippers. The minimum he would have gotten from her was double what he got from me. Kent was an opportunist. He knew my financial situation.

"At the time, I was still working with Debbie. Debbie got to know Kent as a result of his friendship with me. I got to know him before the auction. I think Kent really liked me as a person, and also the fact that I had a 16mm projector. Kent used to love to come over and watch movies. He enjoyed that. I'm sure that I met him within two weeks after he found the shoes.

"He told me he found several pairs. I said, 'Kent, I would give anything to have a pair.' He said, 'You know, the impossible could happen.' He said he knew someone that he had given a pair to, but they weren't into Hollywood memorabilia. He had a pair he might be willing to part with as part of a package deal, including a gingham dress. I got them from Kent as part of a deal.

"I don't think there was ever another person," Shaw added. "I think he did it to make me feel he had to negotiate. I think he was trying to mask the fact that he had all the shoes. I made the deal with Kent before the auction. We settled on a price, he came up with a price, which by today's standards was not much, and a friend of mine loaned me the money. Kent insisted the purchase be made in cash. He brought the shoes and the dress over. I bought them. I had to borrow money. I had to give him the money in cash.

"The day I got mine, when Kent brought them over, I was so thrilled, I literally started crying. Kent hugged me. I was just thrilled to pieces. I told him that if I never owned another possession, I'd be happy.

"Debbie was excited. I said, 'You know, Debbie, everything I get will probably go into the museum.' If Debbie got the idea that those shoes were supposed to go to her, it's because of my involvement with the museum. And she repays me with these stories. If you ever talk to Debbie Reynolds, you can tell her I will burn the ruby slippers before I give them to her."

* * *

"Well," Debbie said, "that's a very intellectual statement. I have no response to something that is given to me as a retort and which I'm unknowledgeable about. If he's angry, he's got the wrong person to be angry with. I've been nothing but nice to him. I don't know why he is angry with me and if he is, I don't care, because he has no right to be."

The reason for a feud was as obvious as it was ugly, but Reynolds seemed to adopt the moral high ground of the vanquished, while

Shaw groveled to defend the spoils of victory. Surely, Reynolds could not say the shoes were hers, yet she made no pretense about wanting a pair.

"I wish I had a pair," she said. "I would be interested in purchasing a pair or trying to save a pair for the museum. I'm not interested for me, Debbie Reynolds. I'm interested for the museum. I would think whoever owns a pair, like Mike Shaw, would want to loan them to a museum."

* * *

"What museum?" Shaw exclaimed. "There is no Hollywood museum. If she had followed the advice of qualified people, her project would have gotten off the ground. We used to go to so many places and she would expect things to be given to her because she was Debbie Reynolds. But I wasn't just going to *give* her the ruby slippers. If there was a Hollywood museum, I would strongly consider making a loan, with nothing more than a simple plaque saying 'from the collection of Michael Shaw' and dedicated to the memory of my parents. But just give them to her? They would never be seen.

"It's my feeling that Kent may have reneged on a deal with Debbie, and he used this story to cover up his embarrassment. At the time all this was going on, Kent wanted to maintain a low profile."

Hadn't Shaw thought about possible recriminations for receiving stolen property?

"None of us had any idea how much the shoes would sell for. The way Kent put it, you didn't think of him stealing. I don't think anyone raised an eyebrow about him taking anything. Nobody cared. He didn't make any clandestine visits to the lot at night. He went in the morning with empty duffel bags, left with full ones, walked right past the guard. They knew that Kent was taking things out for himself. Evidently there was no problem. I assumed it was their way of saying 'thank you.' I didn't feel I was buying a stolen pair."

I asked if he and Kent had ever had a falling out.

"No, we did not have a falling out. He was working on business deals with Debbie and I did not want to be involved. I was nothing but grateful to him. But, all of a sudden, the things that Kent told me didn't make sense.

"It all started with John LeBold. John had this incredibly huge costume collection, long before I was collecting. I don't think any of them knew each other prior to the MGM auction. John wheedled himself in during the retail sale. I went over to Debbie's house one evening, and there was John sitting in her living room. Something began to alert me that I was dealing with some very dishonest people."

* * *

John LeBold was not a new name to me. Kent's old roommate, David, had mentioned him. The connection, David thought, had begun with Debbie Reynolds.

"She was very intent on collecting costumes and memorabilia," David said. "Kent was pleased with what she was trying to do."

There was no question in my mind that Kent had recognized opportunity in Debbie Reynolds. She had spent so much money at the auction that she became an obvious target of Kent's affection and service. She was rich and he had costumes; both wanted to preserve Hollywood's history. Their's was a match made somewhere near heaven.

Kent mined the best of the best from MGM. Certainly, he gave many fine pieces to the auctioneers, but when he found doubles of famous costumes, he kept the best. The perfect example was the ruby slippers, and Reynolds was not shy about her desire for a pair. But things had to be done "del-i-cately," as the Wicked Witch of the West croaked to Dorothy.

If the auctioneer, David Weisz, didn't know about the extra shoes — and Richard Carroll swore he didn't — then the shoes had to be sold quietly. Kent knew that Shaw was working for Debbie and that the two of them attended the sales together. Shaw became the obvious medium.

"Kent said he gave them to Michael because Michael said he was going to give them to Debbie," David told me. "If Michael got those prime items, it was thought he would funnel them to Debbie. There was a lot of buying and selling. They traded that way."

Kent made sure that the pair Shaw received were the best, second only to his. Kent wanted "the museum" to have a very good pair of the ruby slippers. But Shaw had bought the slippers with his own money. He had assumed all the risk, and when he didn't give the slippers to Debbie, who could say a word? It probably took Kent several years to realize what happened.

I believed Shaw. If there had been a museum, he probably would have loaned or donated the ruby slippers he had purchased from Kent. But the Debbie Reynolds museum did not exist, so there was no reason for Shaw to turn the pair over to Debbie. I think that Debbie agreed, which is why she maintained no feud with Shaw. Their situation has yet to be resolved, and in a funny way, their true intentions could only be measured upon the establishment of a Hollywood museum.

Hard feelings clearly existed among Reynolds, Shaw and Warner, so it was no surprise that Reynolds found a new curator for her museum to replace Michael Shaw. That was John LeBold, who turned out to be an old friend of Kent's.

"Kent knew John before I met him," David said. "Kent gave John a Marilyn Monroe dress. It may have been from *The Seven Year Itch*. I think it's in the Debbie Reynolds collection. The things Kent got for John to give to Debbie," David said. "They believed in her effort. A lot of people laid themselves on the line for Debbie Reynolds."

* * *

"RUN, TOTO, RUN"

In the shady world of Hollywood memorabilia, Debbie Reynolds claimed she had "bought everything legitimately." Clearly she walked through the shadow of a dark cloud that hung over the heads of those who dealt in the rags of legends. Her involvement with John LeBold illustrated that.

They had met at the MGM auction, she said. "He walked up to me and said, 'We have the same dream. I have no job and I would like to devote my time to creating a Hollywood museum.' I took him on to help me to preserve my costumes. He had bought quite a few [costumes], but of course he didn't have the money I had, and he started to work for me in 1970."

Officially, LeBold succeeded Michael Shaw and became the curator of the proposed Debbie Reynolds museum. The association between him and Reynolds lasted for a decade. His job description called for both preservation and acquisition. LeBold spent countless hours at Debbie's home, identifying, cataloging, mending, and protecting the pieces in her collection. To be near them was exquisite. He played with them, and they became part of his soul.

With an eye toward acquisition, LeBold spent much of his tenure researching wardrobe inventory at several of the major studios.

Reynolds had persuaded the owners of Columbia, Fox, Paramount, MGM and Warner Brothers to let her into their wardrobe departments, to go through the inventory in search of important costumes. She promised help in cataloging the wardrobe, which no studio had ever done adequately; and she would pay for the work. In return, she asked for donations of, or the opportunity to purchase, certain items. Nearly all the major studios allowed her to come in. John LeBold did the work for $180 a week.

At one point, Reynolds met directly with then Burbank Studios president Robert Hagel, hoping that the studio would offer star clothing to the museum effort. "I was allowed to go into Warners and catalog," she maintained, "and they were going to donate to the museum some of their prime, better costumes." As usual, LeBold went in. For months, the diminutive employee worked in damp, cold storage facilities on the old Warner Brothers lot, the home of Bogart, Errol Flynn, and others.

Methodically, he worked through the department, going from stock costumes into the "lock-ups," areas containing wardrobe that hadn't been seen for years.

He devoured the collection, studying its every cloth, cataloging the stitch of each seam, the color of thread, the designer, the film, and the star who wore it. He wrote all this information on a card and filed it in his head. LeBold studied the Warner collection for several months. By all accounts he was respected. Then the bomb dropped, and the bottom fell out of the underground Hollywood memorabilia business.

* * *

On December 27, 1979, Sergeant Robert Kight of the Burbank Police Department paid a visit to the Debbie Reynolds Professional Rehearsal Studio, on Lankershim Boulevard in North Hollywood.

The DR Studio was the rehearsal home of many young kids aspiring to careers in show business. Actors and dancers went to the large warehouse-sized building in the San Fernando Valley to take sweaty classes offered by the famous singer and actress. But the DR Studio was also the repository of her memorabilia, and the place where John LeBold came to work.

Sergeant Kight went to the studio after the Burbank Studios had reported to the police that some of their costume inventory had been stolen. There he investigated the complaint.

Six days later, Kight returned with a search warrant, which he served at the studio address — 6514 Lankershim. There police confiscated 667 costumes and props allegedly stolen from Warner Brothers and the Burbank Studios between November, 1978, and January, 1980. LeBold was booked as the suspected thief.

* * *

The idea of a Hollywood legend employing an individual who allegedly dealt in stolen memorabilia should have been front-page news in Hollywood. But neither of the trade newspapers, *The Hollywood Reporter* or the *Daily Variety*, reported the scoop. In fact, the story was hardly mentioned anywhere, except in the *Pasadena Star News*. Surely, this was a bigger story, I thought.

I called the Burbank Police Department and asked for Sergeant Robert Kight. He answered his own phone.

"Sure," he said, "I wrote the warrant. Two locations were searched. One was on Lankershim, in Debbie Reynolds' building; the other was his home. She wasn't involved. Debbie Reynolds doesn't have anything to do with it. She had a good reputation. The guy did work for her. She had taken him under her wing. The guy was a fanatic. But as far as I got, she was never under any suspicion or involvement."

More than a year after his arrest, John LeBold was formally charged, by the Los Angeles County District Attorney's office, with receiving stolen property, a violation of Section 496 of the California Penal Code, a felony.

* * *

At his preliminary hearing, Jack Delaney was the prosecution's key witness against LeBold. He was the head of the wardrobe department at the Burbank Studios, having worked on the lot since the days of Jack Warner, and had years of experience and intimacy with the Warner Brothers costume collection. Delaney pointed the finger at LeBold.

Delaney was asked if he "became aware at some time that Mr. LeBold was involved in some sort of venture with regard to setting up a motion picture memorabilia museum?"

"I am sure I was aware," he said. "Yes."

"Were you ever contacted by Mr. LeBold with regard to that?" asked the court.

"Yes, I was. Mr. LeBold was given permission to come to the studio several years ago... and to go through our wardrobe department. He spent most of his time in what we call old Stage 20... in the far corner of the lot and approximately two blocks away from the main wardrobe department. Mr. LeBold at that point went through our wardrobe, selecting what we termed loosely a star wardrobe.

"He had two people working with him, and he spent several months selecting wardrobe, tagging it, identifying it, looking at the labels and putting it on a rack.

"He was not given permission to remove any of the wardrobe. And it was up to the Burbank Studio at some point to make the determination whether to sell, donate, give this wardrobe to a museum that was planned or possibly to auction it off.

"Subsequently it was decided not to do any of these things, and Mr. LeBold and his people working with him were told not to come in the studio any more, and the wardrobe that he had selected and put on these racks, there must have been possibly 20, 25 racks, remained there at that time, at least to my knowledge..."

Delaney was then questioned by LeBold's attorney, Michael Fogel:

"Mr. Delaney, does Burbank Studios have a regular inventory of all the costumes kept there?"

"Not really," answered Delaney. "At one time when we had a much larger staff it was possible to maintain an inventory. But that entry is not exact and really is not kept up because of the large flow of wardrobe in and out. There really isn't an inventory... "

"And all the dresses you identified as coming from Burbank Studios… how did you identify all of those at the time that you saw them?"

"Looked at the labels."

"Do you have a recollection of having seen all of those costumes at one time or another in the Burbank Studios?"

"No, I couldn't say that I would recall having seen all of them."

"So your identification was merely by the label of Warner Brothers in each one?"

"Yes."

As evidence, the prosecution submitted a black silk dress worn by Joan Crawford in *The Damned Don't Cry*, which had an estimated value of $10,000. It was one of the items that Sergeant Kight had confiscated from LeBold at the Debbie Reynolds Studio.

* * *

On February 5, 1981, LeBold's trial began. LeBold's attorney knew that his best defense was that Jack Delaney had previously testified that Warner Brothers maintained no inventory of wardrobe. How could they claim something was stolen if they didn't know what was there?

The prosecution countered by asking how LeBold could have come into the possession of so many costumes clearly marked as Warner Brothers property. LeBold testified that he had purchased many of the costumes from the MGM auction in 1970. He claimed that for years, the studios had traded costumes back and forth, depending on production needs, and that MGM had in its possession, at the time of the auction, many costumes that originally belonged to Western Costume, 20th Century Fox, United Costume, and Paramount, as well as Warner Brothers, in their vast collection. As a witness, LeBold's attorney called Sheila O'Brien, a former wardrobe department employee at MGM. She corroborated LeBold's claim.

"The primary problem with the case," Sergeant Kight said, "was that the record-keeping at the Burbank Studios came down to one dedicated man who knew where everything was but had no inventory. Due to lack of documentation, we were unable to prove beyond a reasonable doubt that LeBold had committed a crime."

On March 25, 1981, the 49-day-old trial ended in a hung jury, with a majority in favor of conviction. The next day the Court declared a mistrial, and on July 16, 1981, the case was dismissed at the request of the Burbank Studios. Of the 667 items confiscated, only 26 were returned to LeBold, including Sally Field's *Flying Nun* hat. The remaining items were returned to the Burbank Studios.

"The guy didn't deserve to go to state prison," said Kight. "He wouldn't have survived it. He just had a fetish about clothes." Kent Warner's name didn't come up at the LeBold trial, but Sergeant Kight was familiar with it and believed that LeBold and Warner were acquainted. "It's a circle that I'm uncomfortable with," he shuddered. "It's just goofy. It's all part of that show-biz shit. I can only compare it to guys who want Rembrandts or Van Goghs."

* * *

At Christie's, Julie Collier was well aware of the problems plaguing those collectors and dealers seeking to buy or sell Warner Brothers movie memorabilia.

"There was a problem with them recently," she told me. "It wasn't here, but over at Sotheby's. I guess Warner Brothers blocked a sale, or at least tried to block a sale. I don't know what happened but we're really careful with Warner Brothers material.

"This whole movie memorabilia business is a little crazy," she said. "There's no way to tell if something's been stolen, because so much was thrown away or traded. We almost have to go by ownership."

Julie pointed out that movie companies like The Burbank Studios wouldn't be coming after their memorabilia if it weren't worth money. "It's not like they all of a sudden care about history," she said. "And the people who saved the stuff are just beginning to reap lucrative benefits." Regardless, she said she stayed away from Warner

Brothers' costumes, unless the consignor had positive proof of ownership.

* * *

"I think he was a very lucky boy to get off," Debbie Reynolds said about John LeBold's trouble with the law. "He took advantage of my friendship. All we were in there for was to be like students and assist in cataloging their inventory and trying to make things organized. That was all. I guess there were so many beautiful things that John became a little involved, more involved than he should have been.

"I certainly didn't realize — I did not know he was bringing things into my studio. I work all year on the road, 42 weeks a year, and certainly I'm not aware of those things. I don't know that he actually took anything. Somehow along the way he lost his dream of a Hollywood museum and it became a business. I have never lost my dream of a Hollywood museum. I'm not going to blame anything on anybody. It's over. He does not work for me.

"I've had a lot of problems," Reynolds admitted, "and that makes me very sad. With all of these would-be savers who were interested in the museum, and now it seems they're much more interested in 'borrowing' my costumes and selling them through other sources. I've had so many things stolen from me. Someone stole twenty boxes of my memorabilia."

"Did you file a police report?" I asked.

"No," she snapped. "I didn't file a report. I didn't file anything. It was just gone. I knew I'd never get it again. Someone made very good hauls. I felt it was an inside robbery, and I didn't want to get anybody in trouble."

* * *

There was one more issue I wanted to settle with Reynolds, and I began by asking her about the movie studios. She knew the old system. Did they care about their history, about their memorabilia? And was that a justification for people like Kent?

"Well, they didn't care, but then again, you shouldn't steal. I went in and bought my things legitimately and they're still mine, and I will keep them and I will one day have a museum. Perseverance will allow. I firmly believe we will have a museum. I never stole from anyone. I have too much integrity for that. Once you believe in a cause you do it and don't become a weak, inconsistent liar about it; have some integrity."

I continued to press on her business with Kent.

"I don't remember that I bought things from Kent," she said. "I bought some things from a couple who used to live in Hollywood that John LeBold took me to see. They had a Charlie Chaplin doll I bought that they said was theirs and I didn't question them, and I paid good money for their costumes.

"I always called Kent and asked him when the slippers would be sold, if he would sell them to me. He said 'yes.' I wasn't there to offer more money when he sold them. I tried to reach Kent. I heard he was ill, and I tried to get through to him when he was sick. I knew he would have sold them to me. He respected me. But I didn't. You know, I'm not going to be pushy and go over to somebody's house on their deathbed."

I then returned to her own boast that Kent had given her the Arabian slippers.

"How did you get the test pair?" I asked.

"Kent Warner," she said, in a testy manner.

"He gave them to you?" I asked.

Her voice turned ice cold. "I bought them," she said.

＊ ＊ ＊

A freaky turn of fate led me to the St. James's Club on Sunset Boulevard. Formerly the Sunset Towers, this elegant old building had once been the sight of garish Hollywood parties before falling into disrepair during the 1970s. It was vacant for a long time, spoiling an otherwise perfect view of the Los Angeles basin. Somebody decided to restore the building to its past glory, a redux job replete with concrete Deco palm trees, where the in-crowd could gather for another fifteen minutes.

I was there for a party. At the edge of a garden patio where I could watch other people arrive, a man stepped into my comfort zone and said a pleasant hello. He was short, thick and smiling under a slick spot of sun-bleached hair. He made conversation about the weather, and in no more than five minutes got me talking about the ruby slippers.

"I have a pair," he said, like a trucker dropping a cigarette butt. It was that offhand. "Sure," I thought. "Whatever you say." I can't tell you how many times I'd heard that, right from the very beginning. I had heard Liza Minelli had a pair, and her sister, Lorna Luft, and Sammy Davis, Jr.; the same with Ray Bolger, Jack Haley and Bert Lahr, and even Gene Kelly and half a dozen other stars. By this time I'd talked seriously to more than 200 people about the slippers, and at least ten of them had claimed to own pairs of ruby slippers. Slipper sightings had been everywhere. On Hollywood Boulevard, in shopping malls, clock stores, museums, bedrooms, living rooms and foyers. Slippers everywhere. By these accounts, Judy Garland must have had forty pair. I figured to find no more than seven. But the last place I figured I'd find a pair was at this party.

But the fellow persisted. "Let me introduce you to my wife," he said. Her name was Rikki Roberts and she had worked at MGM for her mother at the time of the auction in 1970. Most interesting of all, she remembered Kent. But she retreated quite a bit when I asked her if she owned a pair of the slippers. "A pair has been preserved," she said, "and will be offered to one of Judy Garland's children when the time is right." I got the feeling I was hearing more drivel.

* * *

THE BLOND BOMBSHELL

John LeBold's address and phone number were part of the Superior Court Record. I called him on a cloudless California morning. "I'm searching for the ruby slippers," I said. "I understand you knew Kent Warner."

"Ah," he responded. " 'The Keeper of the Shoes.' I knew him for about 20 years." He spoke to me with resignation, as if he had nothing to hide, open and willing.

LeBold said he became a major player in the Hollywood memorabilia business almost by accident. "I don't know why I had to have all those clothes," he said. He had more than 5,000 costumes at the height of his collecting. When the clothes became valuable, he began to sell them, bit by bit. A childhood passion had turned into a marginally profitable, subsistence living.

"When I was a kid I collected photographs and posters from the movies. One day a friend of mine found a suit, a three-piece checked suit that had John Wayne's name in it. He said 'John will love this.' He knew I loved movies. I was in the hospital so he brought it as a gift. It was from the movie *Pittsburgh*. I thought, wow, there's something else to collect besides stills!

"I went back to the store where he found it and found Marlene Dietrich's costume from the same movie. It dawned on me: Here's a set of costumes for the same people in the same movie. That must have been in 1951. I started collecting."

LeBold said the costumes made him feel good. He never considered them as a source of money. If anything, they drained him of every penny he earned. He worked in a book store for $60 a week and spent it all, borrowed against his paycheck and spent more, for costumes he wanted, costumes he had to have.

Sometimes he would find them in used clothing stores for a dollar, or for less. The people who sold them didn't know what they were, nor did they care. If they found out that Greta Garbo had worn a hat and it was something fancy, the price might go up, perhaps to five dollars. Movie costumes in the 1950s and 1960s were that kind of a business. John was one of a very few people who really cared. He knew that everything Garbo wore was designed by Adrian, and that was part of Hollywood's golden history. And for $5, the history was his.

LeBold would make the rounds every evening after work. He didn't drive, so sometimes he rode the bus with arm loads of costumes. Costumes literally dragged in the gutter when he'd get on or off a bus. People must have thought him crazy, this little, fair-skinned man, so shy, so intent on having those clothes.

LeBold's favorite haunts were Logan's Costumes on Melrose Avenue, and Nina's on Western. Logan, he said, was a huge man, unusually tall, "maybe seven feet." Nina was an old woman who made a living off second-hand clothing. Both stores bought seconds from various studio wardrobe departments, who treated the garments as hand-me-downs. A department head might order the clearing of this or that closet, and costumes were either thrown out or sold for rock-bottom prices. Sometimes they were sold by the studio, other times by costumers, who couldn't stand the thought of relegating perfectly good clothing to the trash bin. Nina and Logan bought these lots of clothes for pocket change, then sold them individually, like packs of cigarettes.

John visited both stores regularly, whipping through hangers with fast fingers and clever blue eyes. He looked for labels, and found them. Twentieth Century-Fox, Paramount, Universal, Columbia, Warner Brothers, United Artists, MGM, RKO, along with Western Costume and United Costume. When he found a label, he went to work, hoping to identify the movie the garment had been worn in and the name of the person who had worn it. If the name was that of a star, LeBold had hit pay dirt, even if he didn't know it then.

Often LeBold would find a costume, buy it for a few dollars because of a label, then study it for days, weeks, even years, to learn its identity. Costumes were his jigsaw puzzle, his solitaire, his poker game; they allowed his mind to play. He'd feel the costumes to see if they reminded him of a scene, then he'd go to his books, and then to the stills he had begun collecting as a child.

LeBold had many more movie stills than he had costumes, enough pictures to fill 25 filing cabinets. Matching costumes to stills in his collection became LeBold's passion. It made him feel good to hold the costume in his hands and look at the picture, and it gave him the satisfaction of putting the final piece in a jigsaw puzzle. He could step back out of his own world and imagine himself, for a moment, in a different one. The bright, wonderful world of movies. In this fashion, he was a participant.

Once at Logan's he found a gray coach gown made of light corduroy. It was on the floor and people were walking on it.

"What's this," LeBold asked an old woman tending the store. When she said, "Just an old dress," he said, "Aren't you going to pick it up? People are walking on it." "Oh later," she said, but LeBold grabbed it.

"It was a wonderful gown," he recalled. He could feel it. Old-plantation style, sized for a fine young woman and not old enough to be Civil War vintage. Worn by an actress in a period piece. All this he could feel. He opened the dress inside out and found the *SELZNIK* label with "Scarlet" written on it.

"They didn't even know," LeBold said. "Nobody else had looked at the label. "What do you want to sell it for," he asked, and the old woman said "$50."

He took the dress home and identified it quickly as being from the scene in *Gone With the Wind* in which Vivien Leigh goes to town before the burning of Atlanta, the near-rape scene, which lasted for 30 minutes. It was a major costume from the movie.

* * *

Ironically, it was LeBold's passion for movie stills, not costumes, that had introduced him to Kent Warner. Their first meeting came in the mid-1960s, and it was not friendly.

"I met this boy, Ron Wind, and he said he had to sell his stills. He had a collection of Hollywood photographs — a wonderful collection of slides in a case. I went over to his house to see them, and was sitting there in the living room when this blond bombshell walks in and says, 'Who is he? Get him out. I want dinner.' That was Kent. He was not crazy about house guests.

"Ronny apologized, but I had to leave. Ronny would do anything for Kent, he was so in love with him. The reason he was selling his stills was so Kent could buy something. Anything that Ronny had, he'd sell, and buy something Kent wanted. Like the dining room set — it was Ronny's; Ronny loved it but Kent hated it, so Ronny sold it and Kent bought a new one. Kent drove Ronny to a fever; he was selling things all the time to please Kent. Kent never gave anything. That's the way it was with them.

"Kent was the greediest person I ever met. I was always grateful he was stealing — he certainly saved costumes that would have been thrown away — but his greed got the better of him. He would steal a dress and sell it to buy a chandelier. But a lot of things were saved like that.

"Ronny and Kent got caught a lot. They never really confided in me too much, but I know they got in trouble. Kent was caught going out of a studio with stuff.

"I think it was Ronny who got Kent into collecting costumes. They were both costumers, but Ronny started first. Kent was the one who saw the value in them. I'll say one thing for him, he had... the best things, and only the best. He collected the *crème de la crème*.

"Kent was the type of person who, if he walked by and saw a crown sticking out of a garbage can, he would look at it to see if it had any value. Kent was smart that way. He was always a nice young man. But

I was Ronny's friend, not Kent's. It took him years to accept me. Until the MGM auction — then it was like we were old friends. He liked me then. That's when he really began his collecting."

* * *

"BRING ME THE BROOMSTICK OF THE WICKED WITCH OF THE WEST"

When Kent Warner took the job of cataloging and preparing the MGM star wardrobe for auction in 1970, he walked into work knowing exactly what was going to happen. From that position he was able not only to walk off with the ruby slippers, but to funnel priceless costumes to other collectors, including Michael Shaw, John LeBold and Debbie Reynolds.

In terms of costumes available, the "star" wardrobe auction and the few other feature costume sales were just the beginning. Almost everything in the entire MGM wardrobe collection was slated for retail sale.

The morning after the ruby slippers had sold for $15,000, Kent was fully aware of the sale's significance. People wanted to buy the clothes, not because of what they were or how they were made, but because of who had worn them. Of the countless stars being sold that day, Jeanette MacDonald, for example, was an auction favorite. It was a concept that the auctioneers didn't fully understand.

"Why would people want a Jeanette MacDonald dress?" Richard Carroll asked me. Her fans had come from around the country, groups of them together, to buy her dresses for hundreds of dollars, or maybe one of her hats. Carroll was amazed.

He had expected the finer gowns, the garments made of the best fabrics, stitched by the most gifted hands, or beaded with expensive glass, to be the staple merchandise of the auction; obvious "star" pieces, such as the ruby slippers, might sell for more, but he was sure that the real value of the collection would be in *haute couture*. Why

Jeanette MacDonald, he couldn't imagine. He didn't readily recognize the value of memories. Kent did.

The ruby slippers were not worth $15,000 because they had all those god-awful sequins that kept spilling off the heels in rows; they were worth the money because Judy Garland had worn them. They were worth the money because of "Somewhere Over the Rainbow" and "There's No Place Like Home," because of words that meant memories. Kent realized the true value of the slippers and other costumes was not to be found on a bargain table, but in the memories evoked by those items.

Kent understood what the Jeanette MacDonald fans wanted and for every one of them, there was a fan for Leslie Caron, Susan Hayward, Errol Flynn, Clark Gable, Jean Harlow, Norma Shearer, Elizabeth Taylor — the list went on and on. In Kent's mind, these were the greats of Hollywood and their movie clothes were valuable memorabilia.

Throughout the auction process, these costumes were treated with the respect that Kent and other costumers felt they deserved. But only a small fraction of the vast MGM wardrobe sold under spotlights; the remainder went retail.

* * *

Richard Carroll had convinced David Weisz that a retail sale would be the only swift way to liquidate so much clothing. In measuring the market for so many costumes, Carroll had to figure who would be most likely to buy the MGM clothes. "Old ladies weren't going to buy that stuff," he had said. It would be the kids.

In May of 1970, the fashion trend that gripped the nation belonged to a generation of "hippies." Such was the sale that Carroll envisioned. If David Weisz wanted to liquidate the wardrobe collection as quickly as possible, Carroll said, he should have a "hippie" sale. And that's what David Weisz did.

This disposition of the wardrobe left MGM's costumers very depressed. "It was a very sad time," said Trudy Gellert, who worked in the wardrobe department when the auctions began. "They would come and take racks of clothing and wheel them off to the stage."

"There was nothing we could do about it," said Kyla Magege, a former wardrobe department head and employee. "It just happened."

Rikki Roberts, the woman I met at the St. James's Club with the smiling man, called the retail sale "a stupid idea."

What did Richard Carroll say about that? "Everybody had a better idea about how to sell the costumes," he said, and he vented his frustration by walking out on the retail sale before it began. "I'd just had enough of it," he recalled. But Carroll's idea proved chillingly accurate.

* * *

The specter of a "hippie" sale terrorized Kent, but rather than quit the job, as Carroll and some costumers did, Kent went into action.

In between feature auctions, Kent prepared for the retail sale by feverishly going through rack after rack, bin after bin, searching out costumes worn by important stars. When he found something of value, he put it aside. Meticulously he eyed costumes for familiarity and for their labels.

Labels were what people wanted, labels were worth the money, labels with movie star names. In the movie business, wardrobe department personnel marked every stitch of clothing seen on film with the actor or actress's name. For every film that Betty Grable made, for example, there were maybe 20 or 30 changes of dresses and blouses that she wore.

Because movies are rarely shot completely in sequence—the completed picture is a miracle of editing—the costumer's job is to give the director a complete wardrobe that maintains visual continuity. If an actress wore a necklace with a certain dress in two different scenes, the costumer had to make sure that the necklace and dress appeared in both, even though the amount of time that passed between shooting the two scenes could be weeks. For this reason, labels were attached to everything.

In coats, dresses, pants and blouses, the labels were often stitched into the lining; accessories were usually tagged with safety pins. Once a costume was assembled, the costumer kept it all together on one hanger, or several hangers lashed together. The coat with the skirt, the dress with the belt, the vest with the pants, the shoes, shirt, tie and cuff links, or pearls and earrings, all had to be attached and kept together for continuity. Pinned to the entire outfit was, usually, a production number and the name of the actor, and at times, a hand-written list of scenes.

Kent found many of these costume packages covered with years of dust, and sometimes suffering from deterioration. He searched through these costumes looking for labels and found some great ones.

Occasionally, he found garments with two or three star names. One green velvet dress with mink cuffs had been worn by Judy Garland in *Presenting Lily Mars*, an MGM film, then later by Susan Hayward in *The President's Lady*, which was shot at Twentieth Century-Fox. This was a prime example of John LeBold's contention that studios crossed stock.

Another costume Kent found was a pantsuit that had been worn by Ginger Rogers in *Weekend at the Waldorf*, and later by Marilyn Monroe. Both names were written on labels that had been sewn into the lining.

The best items would end up in the feature auctions, and that was fine with Kent—people paying good money for costumes would have an eye toward their preservation—but something had to be done to save so many treasures from the retail sale, from the grubby, uncaring hands of the masses.

There was also the matter of "doubles" and "triples." Kent, for example, did not find just one of Dorothy's blue-and-white gingham dresses from *The Wizard of Oz*. He found at least ten. Many were test dresses, and all were designed by Adrian. The auctioneers would get one, but what would happen to the rest? Very quietly, Kent told friends, like Michael Shaw, to hold off on buying at the auction, to wait for the retail sale, when duplicates of many famous pieces would be sold with less fanfare.

Kent kept certain important costumes aside, costumes that deserved the appreciation of a collector who would preserve them. Under such conditions, the retail sale opened at the end of May, 1970.

* * *

Richard Carroll may not have known the full value of Hollywood costume memorabilia, but he knew merchandising extremely well. True to his prediction, kids — teenagers and college students — dominated the retail sale, and within a matter of weeks, the entire MGM wardrobe collection was liquidated.

But also true to Kent's prediction, the retail sale was a madhouse. He retched at the sight of kids trampling through decades of Hollywood memorabilia. He watched them take dresses and talk about how they would tear off the lace and sew it to blue jeans; he looked pained while ignorant children soiled garments that once belonged to the biggest stars of the big screen. He couldn't stand watching so much movie history become nothing more than thrift shop property.

* * *

Chris Rich was a bored 18-year-old in the summer of 1970, when she and her sister decided to check out the MGM wardrobe sale. By the time Chris arrived, the sale had been on for weeks and would last just a few more days. "They were clearing out everything," she remembered.

"We went into this big warehouse where they had all the clothes on racks. On a rack full of coats I found this jacket I liked. It was a sailor-type jacket. I picked it up, then put it back, then picked it up again an hour later.

"It wasn't until a woman walked up to me that I realized what I had picked up. The woman had been reading labels and asked me if

I had been reading labels. I hadn't. But when I looked for one in this coat, I was surprised."

The label she found read:

May 1935 Especially Made for:
Clark Gable
Brown & Herman
760 S. Hill Street Los Angeles

The jacket she picked up was the Royal Navy coat Gable had worn in *Mutiny on the Bounty* (1935).

"Everything was selling for just a dollar," Chris said. "I thought they made a boo-boo. The lady looking at labels offered me $20 right there if I would give her the coat. I said no and took it to the counter."

Chris was one of the few who recognized the value of her possession. She kept the coat until recently, when she sold it through a newspaper ad for $2,000.

* * *

"A CLINKING, CLANKING, CLATTERING COLLECTION OF CALIGINOUS JUNK"

John LeBold vividly recalled the retail sale and Kent's efforts to save costumes.

"What they did at that place was so sad, so criminal," he said. "It was awful. People were pushing, grabbing, shoving. There were derelicts, in off the streets, looking for cheap clothes, and the people running the sale didn't care. 'Let's make money,' they said. They had no feeling.

"There would be, say, a Greta Garbo outfit on the racks, with everything attached, just like the costumer had just brought it back from the set. They would have the gown, the sleeves, the petticoat, the hat, the gloves, the boots, all intact. When the auctioneers came in they separated everything. All the attachments were sold separately. The petticoats went onto a pile of petticoats, the shoes into a bin of shoes. It was like a grocery store.

"The auctioneers opened up the stages and just sold things to kids. You cannot believe the emotion of seeing... it was like Macy's at a white sale. Thousands of ladies showing up and pulling at things, and here there were priceless, precious things that these beatniks were grabbing to wear on the street. You know, everybody was wearing those flashy costumes, Sergeant Pepper and all that stuff. I could see things, headdresses being walked out for 10, 15, 25 bucks. Beautiful costumes that were worn by Robert Taylor, Gary Cooper — it was horrendous for me.

"Kent was very interested in preserving the costumes. If something was falling apart or decaying, he'd try to save it. Kent made sure people who would preserve things got costumes, including the ruby slippers. He said, 'I don't want these kids to see these things and destroy them.'

"They kept it very hush-hush that there were other costumes because people would not have spent money at the auction if they knew there was going to be a sale after the auction for the exact same things they were buying. Why buy a gingham dress of Judy Garland's from *The Wizard of Oz* at a thousand dollars when you could probably pick it up for fifty to one hundred, or three hundred on a rack?

"I wish I could re-live it," LeBold said. "Back then, I didn't know what I was doing. Nobody really did." Except Kent.

"Kent told me there were things in the back that he had saved and would give me first look at. What he would do is point me in the right direction and I would pull things and put them on my rack."

Such as Judy Garland's red velvet dress from *Meet Me In St. Louis*. Kent sold that to LeBold for two hundred dollars. At the time, it was a lot of money. But Kent reminded John that it was a valuable dress. "When he realized these things were valuable he got dollar signs in his eyes." In 1984, the dress sold for $2,750 at auction.

"I bought over 3,000 items. I mortgaged my house to do it. I think a lot of the items were like neckties. I probably picked up about 750 complete costumes. Something like that. I spent about $10,000."

But even Kent could not get his hands on everything that was being sold at the MGM sales. With each new day the auctioneers found more storage areas, more bins of clothes, seven sound stages worth of clothing in all. By the end of June, they were throwing costumes away. While Kent busied himself with the costumes at hand, LeBold made a habit of searching garbage cans.

He found a string of bow ties, a bunch of them lashed together, labeled "Clark Gable." He found the "popcorn" blouse Judy Garland had worn in *Meet Me In St. Louis*. And he found *Marie Antoinette's* crown, worn by Norma Shearer, the one with the music box and the birds that pop out and spin. LeBold called it "my favorite possession."

* * *

While other collectors were specifically interested in one star or another, like the Jeanette MacDonald fans who came from around the country to buy her gowns at the auction, or like Kent, who personally favored Ginger Rogers and Judy Garland, LeBold wanted to collect them all, and dabbled in any star name. Certainly, he had his own favorites, but more than collecting names, he was collecting scenes from movies.

He had a number of Betty Grable costumes, many from the same movies, such as *Meet Me After the Show, The Shocking Miss Pilgrim*, and *Sweet Rosie O'Grady*. From *Daddy Long Legs*, he had four different gowns worn by Leslie Caron. LeBold's collecting defied conventional wisdom. He imagined these gowns displayed on lifelike mannequins and flown from the walls, giving motion to the moment.

LeBold said he had bought many pieces directly from Kent at the auction, and more during the next few years. Their renewed friendship became profitable to both men. LeBold's association with Debbie Reynolds made him one of Kent's favorite customers. He could sell LeBold the costumes for cash in pocket with the belief that they were going to a bona fide Hollywood museum. Those were the magic words, and Kent heard LeBold speak them.

* * *

"Kent believed in the museum. He had a lot of respect for Debbie. She was trying very hard. I know she bought the Arabian test pair from him.

"I was a totally starry-eyed kid at the time of the auction. From what I read in the papers, I knew Debbie was trying to open a museum. I found out where she was sitting at the auction. I wanted to tell her about my collection. I had about 3,500 costumes then. I told her I shared her dream. She said she needed a curator for her collection, someone in place of Mike Shaw, for everything that she was buying at the auction. Before that she had literally nothing. After the auction, I went to work for her."

"For fifteen years she promised, promised and promised. I did everything I could for her, there was nothing I wouldn't do for the woman because I believed in her. Now I think she's a perverse collector."

LeBold recounted Reynolds' efforts to salvage costumes from the studios before they were trashed, how she had approached the presidents of Columbia, Fox, Paramount, MGM and Warner Brothers, asking permission to research their wardrobe stock. The experience was an eye-opener for LeBold.

"I didn't know how to drive at that time. I took three busses to get to Hollywood. Sometimes I spent six months in studios. We started at Columbia, in Gower Gulch. Some days I was there from eight in the morning until 10 p.m. At the end of the period of researching, Debbie would come in and look at the costumes I had put aside, then decide which she wanted to buy. Then she'd make an offer to the studio. They were extremely nice.

"After Columbia, we went to Fox. One time I was at Fox and they took out their entire history of special effects, photo after photo, plan after plan, and filled three huge garbage dumpsters. Textbooks for the future. History. It was starting to rain and I panicked. There was no time. I went all over trying to figure how to save it. I called Debbie, Debbie tried to save it. None of it was saved. Nothing. All ruined." But LeBold did find and save many pieces of Fox wardrobe for Reynolds, including most of Marilyn Monroe's gowns, which Reynolds purchased.

"At Paramount, they told us there was nothing there. Later, I found out from Kent that they pulled out 40 racks of clothes, vintage things, and gave them to the Salvation Army. But they had put some things aside. Paramount was one of the few studios that cared, unlike MGM, which took their entire history of still photos and took them to the dump and saw to it that it was buried. Why not give them to the Academy? A gentleman there allowed us to get a lot of stuff that was being thrown away."

LeBold also remembered spending six months at Warner Brothers. "It was damp and cold, but I never had seen such fabulous things. There were 20 racks, two and three stories high in a room — storage space on a sound stage — with no light, no name tags. I bought a miner's cap with a light to see. I had to pull stills from their movies to identify the costumes. At the end of my research, they had this incredible collection put aside and they decided not to sell it to Debbie. She was very upset.

"Before I went there they didn't know what those costumes were, a blue pinstripe suit was just that. After my work they knew what it was. Later, after my trial, I found costumes in used clothing stores, Warner Brother's costumes, with labels that I wrote. Incredible."

"I was like a scapegoat or something," he said when I asked about Warner Brothers' efforts to prosecute him. "What was so silly is that they were saying I had certain things and other people all over town had the same thing, and they were being sold openly at stores all over the place. What it came down to is that Jack Delaney was trying to protect himself. He didn't want it to be known that the stuff wasn't in the building. After 70 years of business, stock gets mixed up. MGM sold seven warehouses of stock and Warner Brothers is trying to tell me that it was strictly their stock. He didn't have an inventory. It's a very bad spot in my life. It cost me thousands and thousands of dollars and I was proved innocent."

I remembered that Kent had spent a considerable amount of time at Warner Brothers during 1966 and 1967, working as a costumer on *Camelot*. That's where Kent had found Bogart's *Casablanca* trench coat, which he sold to Michael Shaw long before Jack Delaney and The Burbank Studios ever noticed any wardrobe missing. Kent knew what was going on with the studio. Did LeBold talk to him about the indictment?

"I called him and asked if he would testify for me," LeBold said. "He told me he would kill me if I brought him into it. He got very angry with me and never spoke to me again."

* * *

LeBold's association with Debbie Reynolds began when her relationship with Michael Shaw ended, immediately after the MGM auction. LeBold recalled that it had something to do with the ruby slippers and a purple Garbo cape from *Queen Christina*, but specifically, he said, "she never mentioned what happened." All he knew was that Shaw was out and he was in as the curator of her Hollywood museum.

"Kent wanted to make sure she got a pair," LeBold said. "He offered them to me. I don't think he wanted that much, maybe $1,000. He wanted them to go to a museum.

"I was totally green about the shoes at that time. Kent did not clue me in about it and I did not discuss the shoes until probably after the auction and after the sale. They definitely kept it hush-hush.

"There were supposed to be five pairs in existence," he said, the same number Reynolds had remembered. "Kent found them in a dust bin area, lying there. The slippers were going to be thrown out. A couple pairs *were* thrown out and then retrieved. I think he said three pairs. Kent asked, 'should we toss them or should we save them?' The Kerkorian people didn't know what memorabilia was, they only knew what money was." So Kent kept the slippers.

A pair had gone to the auction, and another to Roberta Bauman back in 1940. What about the other pairs?

"He kept a pair," the size 5Bs, I thought, the Witch's shoes, "and he sold a pair to Debbie Reynolds, but she lost them." Those were the 5-1/2s that belonged to Michael Shaw. "And I bought my slippers from Kent, which were stolen. But a lot of things were saved like that."

LeBold's revelation startled me. "You have a pair?" He said: "I bought a pair from him. They were stolen from me. It's very sad. I was saving them for the museum. They were stolen in 1980."

"Do you know who stole them?" I asked.

"I have my suspicions."

* * *

"CURSES, CURSES, SOMEBODY ALWAYS HELPS THAT GIRL"

In all my conversations with Roberta Bauman, our talk rarely focused on the material value of the ruby slippers. She viewed them as a child would, as something special to behold, filled with thoughts of family, friends, and home. But since the MGM auction, she had known that someday her slippers would be sold. This knowledge reminded me that any story about the ruby slippers and their magic could not live only in the past.

The shoes brought calm to Roberta, but she existed within the eye of a hurricane, surrounded by anxious fans and collectors alike, each with a secret dream to own a pair of Judy Garland's magical slippers. My involvement was no longer that of a bystander. She brought me into the perpetual swirl of her delightful dilemma. "I'd like to sell the slippers." she appealed to me, confidentially, "but what do I do?"

Roberta's quandary was laced with satisfaction. "I have had the shoes all these many years and I find it is time to pass them on to others to enjoy. I have shown them to many school children, including my own. They have served my purpose." But for her life, Roberta could "not put a price on this history-making treasure." She didn't care for the money so much as she wanted them to fall into the right hands.

"What do you think I should do?" she asked. "I don't want to get knocked off because of them."

Honestly, I couldn't answer her question. She alone would have to decide their disposition.

"Do you know how much you want to sell them for?" I asked. "Oh my!" she said. The thought of the question bothered her. She was not a collector or a dealer. "I don't know." she said. "How much do you think?"

I knew the benchmark in Roberta's mind had been set long ago, at $15,000. That was the sale price of the slippers in 1970, when it was first revealed that there was more than one pair. She didn't regard her pair as any better or worse than that pair and, for that reason, felt $15,000 was fair.

I didn't know what to think. Charlie Chaplin's bowler hat, cane and floppy shoes had just sold in London for an unbelievable $150,000. How many of those shoes, hats and canes did he have? Did they compare to the ruby slippers? Or "Rosebud," the celebrated sled from *Citizen Kane*. Steven Spielberg had paid $60,000 for one of many replicas made for burning in the movie's final scene. And it wasn't even the original.

Prices for these things were just crazy. A nondescript Marilyn Monroe blouse from *Bus Stop* had recently brought $12,000. These prices defied belief. Yet belief undeniably instills value, and what symbol of belief in all of Hollywood, maybe all America, could be found more potent, more pure, more powerful, more enduring than the ruby slippers? Could such a symbol have a price?

"What about that Texan?" she asked. "Do you think I should call him?" I couldn't say yes or no to that question, either, but my feeling was that a fair market price would not come from a private deal. For all her earthy charm and skill, Roberta was no purveyor of collectible goods, and a shark would certainly take advantage of her. The Texan, who had called me months before, seemed to be an opportunist. Sure, she could make her deal quietly and be rid of her property for cash, but I asked her, "Is that the way you want to sell your slippers?"

"Well, what about an auction?" she said.

I knew she wanted to make the right decision, but she was talking to the wrong person. "Do you want to talk to someone at Christie's?" I asked.

* * *

I mentioned Christie's for several reasons. The venerable auction company, with more than 200 years experience in the business, had recently proved their interest in and respect for Hollywood memorabilia, as evidenced by the advance publicity they gave to such consignments and the prices they received for them. Christie's was a high-profile operation. They also had previously handled a pair of ruby slippers.

I mainly thought of Christie's because of Julie Collier. Julie was a unique individual. She cared about her clients, was loyal to her profession, and recognized the intrigue of the ruby slippers. Even when I asked questions she could not answer because of confidentiality, she remained curious, attentive and helpful.

As supervisor of Christie's Collectibles, a specialized department in the New York house, her primary responsibility was secondary to fine art. Dolls, toys and costumes, the kind of things that grandmothers kept in locked cabinets, this was the area of her expertise. Dolls especially.

Christie's maintained the department because it realized a steady, though marginal, profit in the business of brokering porcelain figurines. Hollywood memorabilia was a stepchild, just as it had been for David Weisz, but it was a stepchild that July Collier warmly embraced.

"I really loved those shoes when we had them." she hummed. "I loved the movie when I was a little girl. Having them right there was fantastic. They were such a mystery."

We were long past the fact that Kent Warner had consigned the size 5B slippers in 1981, a fact she had acknowledged but would never admit. "Of course." she'd say, "I can't confirm that." That's why I respected her. She treated people fairly in terms of business, and warmly as friends.

Most of the time I called Julie to pester her for information, but this time I had some to give. "Roberta Bauman may be ready to sell her pair of ruby slippers." I said.

* * *

It didn't take Roberta more than a week to sign a contract with Christie's. As expected, she found Julie a delight to deal with. In the meantime, I continued with my own search for ruby slippers.

John LeBold's revelation provided one more avenue to explore. Some time back I had heard a rumor from a memorabilia dealer, a guy who mostly swapped posters and lobby cards, that a pair of ruby slippers had been "stolen from a big collection, a major collection."

LeBold certainly had a huge costume collection. And now he was telling me that he had had a pair of ruby slippers that had been stolen. LeBold told me a lot of things had been stolen from his collection. He sounded like Debbie Reynolds. And just like her, he wouldn't name names.

The poster dealer told me "find someone named Bill Thomas. He might have the shoes." That was my only clue.

* * *

"HOW ABOUT A LITTLE FIRE, SCARECROW?"

Curiosity took me into countless second-hand clothing boutiques, as I ventured deeper and deeper in search of Kent Warner and the ruby slippers. I searched the avenues for Kent Warner, hoping to find his legacy in the possessions of so many fashionable shops that specialized in "vintage" clothing and Art Deco, and maybe even an old friend who remembered him.

In these shops, usually lined with racks of clothing against walls that stretched like bowling alleys into the backyards of West Hollywood, I found store owners who were very different from Nina and Logan. They knew the value of the clothes they sold and their prices seemed too high, almost prohibitive. If a dress had a star label, the tag had a star price. "You're buying much more than a gown," they'd say.

I mentioned Kent Warner's name to some shop owners and they cooed, somewhat reverently acknowledging his legacy, which they could now touch, fondle and take to the bank. Kent Warner did not make the memorabilia market — he made the market possible.

Few of these retailers admitted knowing Warner — most didn't — but sometimes they would tell me the names of others, the names of collectors and dealers who might have known Kent. Through this word-of-mouth, I found Bill Thomas. His name was familiar to the owner of the "Retake Room" on Laurel Grove in Studio City. "He sells vacuums in a shop down the street," the lady told me.

I called him immediately and asked the obvious question. "Yes," he answered. "I have a pair."

* * *

This slight beanpole of a man sported a flat-top haircut, wore a button-up shirt, creased blue jeans and black cowboy boots. It didn't take long to learn that Bill Thomas was part of the second generation of Hollywood memorabilia magnates. He made no bones about collecting star wardrobe not just for the love of movies, but for profit. The business, he explained, was fiercely competitive, but still confined to a relatively small number of participants.

Like John LeBold, Bill Thomas was a big player and his face was familiar in these trendy vintage clothing shops; unlike LeBold, he had come late to the stage. As a new kid on the block, he moved in on old territory, which caused a good deal of anger and jealousy among the other dealers and collectors. In a relatively short period of time, Thomas amassed a large collection, which included pieces he had purchased from Kent Warner. He was one of Warner's last customers. "I knew Kent quite well when he died," he said.

* * *

Bill Thomas didn't recall exactly when or where he had first met Kent — it was at either the Ambassador Hotel in December, 1980 or several months later in Paul Tiberio's antique store on Robertson — but he distinctly remembered why they had met: Kent owned a Mae West dress that Thomas wanted to buy.

Kent had the dress up for sale at the Ambassador auction, along with the ruby slippers and other items from his collection. His prices, Thomas said, were extremely high. "I can't remember if he was there or not," Thomas said. "There was some concern about protecting the identity of the owner of the slippers, but I was told Kent owned the dress.

"My first impression of him was not kind, but I enjoyed Kent tremendously. He was a very colorful fellow. Later, I ran into Kent at an Art Deco antique store on Robertson." Tiberio's. "I spoke to him about the Mae West. It was a beautiful, beaded gown she wore in *Every Day's a Holiday*, designed by Schiaparelli. He wanted several thousand dollars for it.

"Paul Tiberio became furious when I purchased the Mae West. I guess he wanted it. Paul and Kent were quite close. When I came upon Kent, a couple other collectors got pissed. We had spats among us, and Kent did his best to keep us apart.

"At that time I was a collector. I merely bought from him. Everything went from word-of-mouth to a handshake. We developed a bond of trust. Our relationship was: I bought, he sold. Mostly, I gave him cash. If I couldn't afford something, I paid him over time. He kept the piece. When I finished paying, he gave it to me.

"When I went over to his house to buy the Mae West there were the ruby slippers and an original test dress, a blue cotton dress with attached sleeves. He was still in his Hollywood apartment. It was very 'Alice in Wonderland.'

"He was very much a collector. His real loves were radios, televisions and cigarette lighters. The costumes were something he picked up in the process. They never really had that much importance to him. The costumes were just a source of income. Of course, the ruby slippers became important and consuming to him. He kept the shoes on a pillar on the landing of the stairs. Later he packed them away.

"He did enjoy Ginger Rogers. He had some of her dresses. He had the 'Piccolino' dress from *Top Hat* and the beaded, crystal sandpaper dress from *Follow the Fleet*. He also had the herringbone coach outfit from the same movie. They were very important to him. I think he cared for her stuff more than Judy Garland's. Either he or his mother donated the 'Piccolino' to the Smithsonian upon his death. The sandpaper dress still hasn't surfaced."

* * *

"I see Kent all the time," Thomas continued. "I do business on Melrose and I see Kent. At the auctions, I see Kent. The fringe dress that Marilyn Monroe wore in *Some Like It Hot* — it went for 18,000 pounds at Christie's in London — came from Kent to Tiberio's to an anonymous buyer to me. I sold it. The red velvet dress Judy Garland wore in *Meet Me In St. Louis*, Kent sold that to a collector, and he sold it to me, and I sold it for $2,750. The Schiaparelli dress from *Every Day's A Holiday*, Kent sold it to me and I sold it in Paris for 14,000 pounds. I've been told that Karl Lagerfeld bought it. In the world of Hollywood memorabilia, Kent is everywhere.

"Kent was the beginning. He was the first to preserve costumes from destruction. We all were there at the dumpsters, we all knew each other, but Kent was probably there first. In the beginning, we watched the studios destroy things. Less than five percent of everything made and worn still exists. So much was destroyed, so much just rotted away. A lot was dumped, burned, buried. There was a story about Lucille Ball when she bought the RKO studio — they buried the entire wardrobe. That's one of the reasons Kent's Ginger Rogers dresses are so rare.

"Kent was quite young when he came to Hollywood. He was into dying and cutting his hair. He came to Hollywood with another man. Kent Warner and Ron Wind... that was a love/hate relationship. I think Kent's mother came between them.

"Ron called her 'Shadow.' Ron and Kent would run away for the weekend. They seemed to go to Palm Springs or San Francisco. They made friends in San Francisco. Wherever they went, lo and behold the phone would ring at four in the morning and Ron would be livid. She and Kent were connected at the hip.

"Ron was also a collector. It was Ron who got Kent going. Ron started with an exhibition of studio costumes, I think it was at the Lincoln Arts Center. That's when the interest began. They both went from there. They were two of a kind when it came to collecting. They got the white palm trees from the Coconut Grove together. One night Ron and Kent went down there and got them and filtered them out to people.

"Then there was *Camelot*. Ron and Kent and Joe Semoruga, they all worked on that film. Kent got a sketch from John Truscott of Richard Harris. That's when a lot of costumes disappeared from Warner Brothers.

"Ron enjoyed the transferring of property; Kent was interested in things æsthetically. Kent had the better eye. They leafed through racks of clothes all their lives, that's how they made a living, how they found things. Ron created the interest in Kent, and Kent took it to MGM."

* * *

Bill Thomas knew Ron Wind very well. During the last year of Ron's life, Bill lived with him, and nursed him, caring for the dying man. Ron often talked about better days and sometimes told stories about Kent. Bill Thomas told them to me.

Though Ron hadn't immediately shared Kent's enthusiasm for vintage costumes, he learned to appreciate and participate in what Kent was saving. Ron's professional career skyrocketed while he lived with Kent. In the costuming department at CBS in Los Angeles, the home of many celebrated variety shows during the 1960s, Ron had worked on shows starring Jonathan Winters, Red Skelton, and Carol Burnett; and on *The Smothers Brothers Show*, where Ron surprised Bette Davis.

It had been nearly 30 years since the legendary actress had starred in a favorite film of Kent's, *The Private Lives of Elizabeth and Essex*. Her co-star was Errol Flynn. When Ron told Kent that she was going to be on the Smothers show, Kent suggested dressing her up in the "Queen Elizabeth" dress. She had done the movie at Warner Brothers, Kent remembered.

Without telling anyone the plan, Ron went to the Warner Brothers wardrobe department and searched for hours, then days. Costumers there could only point him in a direction, but they couldn't tell him exactly where to look. They had no idea if the dress was still there.

Ron found the dress, finally, and took it to the Smothers Brothers sound stage, where he presented it to Bette Davis. She couldn't believe her eyes, which welled with tears. She was Queen Elizabeth again, after three decades. She thanked Ron again and again, and they had a picture taken together. Ron kept it on display at the Stanley house, a wonderful memory. Bill Thomas showed it to me.

* * *

Ron didn't share Kent's enthusiasm for material things. He sold stills, props and costumes for money, and with the money, he paid for his habits. One of them was Kent. There was nothing Ron wouldn't do, wouldn't buy for Kent. The Academy Awards night was one example. Ron had paid for the evening. But his feelings for Kent went much deeper.

One Christmas, shortly after leaving New York, Kent complained about the warm weather in Los Angeles. It didn't feel like Christmas time because there was no snow. With a splendid sense of pleasure, Ron devised a plan. On Christmas Eve, after Kent had gone to sleep, Ron stole out of the house to meet friends. They had rented a truck to drive up to the mountains, where they shoveled a load of snow into the back, then brought it down to Hollywood and covered the front lawn of the Stanley Avenue house. When Kent woke up the next morning, he got his holiday wish: a white Christmas.

Nobody knew exactly how or why Ron and Kent split up but most guessed it had been a combination of clashing personality traits. Ron apparently tired of Shadow and grew intolerant of Kent's occasional philandering. Kent became frustrated and angry with Ron's worst habit, a drug dependency. To friends at Berman's, Kent confessed that Ron was not just selling stills and costumes out of the Stanley house, he was dealing drugs. Kent had to get out before something terrible happened. They split with hard feelings.

More than ever before, Kent needed his work to keep his mind off Ron. He continued to free-lance, working again at Warner Brothers, until a stroke of luck changed the course of his life. The MGM auction began.

* * *

"Kent's first major job was correlating the MGM auction," Bill Thomas said. "The whole time he was at MGM he was looking for wonderful souvenirs. That's when he started pursuing the ruby slippers. He was obsessed. Kent kept asking, 'Where are the shoes?' It was the one thing he wanted, he said. 'If I could have anything, it would be the shoes.'

"Kent told me the story in the late 1970s. He said he found a woman who thought she knew where the slippers were—I knew he had to give a pair of shoes away. They were given to a daughter of a woman who worked at MGM, in exchange for information on where the shoes were. He didn't say the name of the woman. This stuff was kept secret."

"I think Kent was the first person to see the ruby slippers in 30 years. He said they were in an old sound stage called 'the barn,' which was used for storage. It was an old building, missing its roof, three or four levels. MGM stored a lot of older wardrobe on the upper levels. One lady thought they might be up there, but said, 'I wouldn't go up there, it's a very, very dangerous building. Rat-infested.' He found the *Marie Antoinette* costumes up there, found a whole storage for shoes. He started going through everything up there. Everything was covered with dust. The only light was sunlight bleeding through the roof. He found himself in a sea of green shoes. Something caught his eye. He blew away the dust, and there were the ruby slippers. He said he found six pairs. The woman in the South had another pair.

"I don't think David Weisz knew, but certain people at the auction knew. I think they were divided up. Kent had the pair that Judy used to click her heels together three times. They had a leather bottom, lacquered. No orange felt. Most of the ruby slippers were quite scuffed. His shoes had small scratches in a circular pattern on the soles. He kept the shoes because he thought they were neat. His pair were the best, the Witch's shoes.

"He told me there were seven pairs," Thomas offered. This was consistent with the stories Kent had told his roommate David, Don Ritchie, and Ken Maley. Again and again, through all these interviews, I recounted the slippers. The Smithsonian pair — one — which I assumed was the same as the MGM auction pair; Roberta Bauman's — two; the Michael Shaw shoes — three; and Kent Warner's 5Bs, the Witch's shoes — four. That's all I knew about, except for the "Arabian test pair" — five; the "bugle bead" test pair evidently existed, but had not surfaced anywhere — this could be number six.

" — and I have a pair," Thomas said. "But I didn't buy mine from Kent. Mine were given to me as a gift for my 21st birthday. I acquired them eight years ago, from a woman."

* * *

Roberta Bauman's size 6B ruby slippers were shipped from Memphis to New York City on Wednesday, March 9, 1988, via United Parcel Service. They were packaged carefully, stuffed with cotton, and wrapped in individual sleeves inside a clear plastic storage container which was placed in a larger cardboard box. Around the container she had put styrofoam peanuts to keep the cargo from jostling. The box was secured with strapping tape.

Julie Collier gave Roberta instructions for shipping the parcel. "Don't tell them what's in there. Just say it's clothing." The package was insured for $300 and cost Roberta $16.50 for overnight delivery.

As Christie's assumed no liability for property in transit, Roberta suffered an anxious 24 hours. "If anything happened it was my bait," she said, "but I wasn't worried. I had shipped so much before, I have every confidence in UPS. I was sure they would get there all right. Later on, a UPS person said if I had said what they were, they might not have made it to New York."

Julie was equally, if not more anxious, to receive Roberta's package. She wanted to see these ruby slippers. When they arrived, Julie called Roberta with a sigh of relief. "She was so very excited and a little bit speechless to see and touch them," Roberta said. And the excitement level at Christie's was much higher than it had been for Kent Warner's shoes in 1981.

The first matter of business was the reserve. What dollar amount would Roberta reserve as the lowest possible price for her ruby slippers? She asked $15,000, as I knew she would. Like politicians,

Christie's estimated their value with cautious optimism, publicly stating the sale price was expected to be between $15,000 and $20,000.

Auction houses generally like to estimate a little low, but near enough to the closing price to maintain credibility. Their experts couldn't always be right, but they wanted to make sure buyers came with extra money stuffed in their socks, the old school yard trick.

Next, the shoes were photographed for the auction catalog. The picture would go on the cover.

* * *

The deal was finalized on the Ides of March, 1988. A few weeks later I received an invitation in the mail:

*The Board of Directors of Christie's
and
Mrs. Dennis Stanfill
request the pleasure of your company
for cocktails, music and a private preview of
Portrait of Adeline Ravoux
by Vincent Van Gogh
Magnificent Jewels from the Collection of
His Late Royal Highness
Sir Sultan Mohamed Shah Aga Khan III
and Ruby Slippers worn by
Judy Garland in* The Wizard of Oz
*Wednesday, the thirteenth of April
six until eight o'clock
Rodeo Room
Beverly Hills Hotel*

Roberta Bauman certainly was stepping into a fancy room with fine company. Her ruby slippers were being displayed within world-class spitting distance of an old canvas Vincent Van Gogh had painted during his demented, dying days. *Portrait of Adeline Ravoux*, Christie's said, would sell for about twenty million dollars.

It was a shame that Roberta couldn't be at the affair, to see so many stuffed shirts whimsically staring at her ruby slippers. They captured the imagination of those present. In Hollywood, it might have been hard for people to understand the worth of a fine painting, or genuinely to treasure the collective value of so many precious stones. But everybody had a taste of the magic that was the ruby slippers. Michael York and Ed McMahon had their pictures taken while standing next to them.

For Christie's, the evening was a huge success.

* * *

Michael Shaw told me long before Roberta decided to auction her pair of ruby slippers that he would be glad to pay her $2,000 for them, but he insisted they were worth no more. Anybody who thought they would sell for $15,000, he said, was dreaming.

Debbie Reynolds, on the other hand, said Roberta "should get a nice price," but added that she would be unable to bid for them. She wanted an auction catalog anyway.

Roberta asked me time and again during our phone conversations, "How much do you think?" I didn't know, I maintained, but I had my own guess. I shared that with Tod Machin, whose own emotions about the auction were terribly mixed.

For years, Tod had hoped that he might be able to privately purchase the shoes from Roberta, when it was time for her to pass them on. In his wildest dreams, he could only manage a figure of $10,000. He was no rich man.

Tod wanted the shoes for a *Wizard of Oz* museum in Kansas, where he believed the shoes belonged. But these inner thoughts were quieted by his feelings for Roberta. From the moment he had first contacted her, Tod thought of Roberta as his second grandmother. And the sale of the shoes was not a family matter; the best price had to come from an auction. Roberta deserved the best price, Tod thought.

Tod also delighted in speculation. "How much do you think?" he asked me. I couldn't escape the figure of $50,000, that's what I believed. "But wouldn't it be something," I told him, "If they went for $100,000?" Of course, that was too much, even for dreaming.

Julie Collier was much more conservative, having experienced the disappointing sale of Kent Warner's prized 5Bs only seven years earlier. Sure, she entertained thoughts of a six-figure sale, but reminded me that Chaplin's memorabilia had sold high because two bidders were determined to win the auction; they had gone head to head and bowled over the other participants. Privately, though, she hoped for a big sale.

Julie certainly didn't play down expressed interest in Roberta Bauman's ruby slippers. She assured Roberta that the reserve would pass, that interest in the sale of the shoes was growing and growing. And, as I expected, Julie proved to be very protective of Roberta.

"Even up to the night before the auction," Roberta related, "Julie was still calling me to be sure I was all right. She was very specific not to let any person contact me unless she called first to tell me the score. She would not let anyone harass me under any circumstances. I told her I was at peace since I sent the contract and shipped the shoes."

* * *

Publicity far exceeded expectations. National newspapers and network television picked up the story of the sale of the ruby slippers. As anticipation built, potential buyers could only wait for the magical date: June 21, 1988. At 10 a.m., the auction would begin. The slippers were Lot #125 on the auctioneer's schedule.

A pack of television and newspaper reporters staked out opportune seats at the back of the auction room, arriving early that morning. The *CBS Evening News* planned a feature segment. *USA Today* ran a cover story and *Entertainment Tonight* showed up along with reporters from *The New York Times* and the *Associated Press*.

Many people came to watch as Christie's filled their New York sales room to capacity. More than 500 people were there waiting for the appointed hour.

Everywhere, white bidding paddles sprinkled the room; white paddles clutched in the sweaty, nervous palms of bidders. Some had the white paddles stuffed between their knees as they sat in their chairs, others kept them under their arms. White paddles with numbers, assigned to those registered as buyers at Christie's. It was very easy to get a paddle. Name, address, Social Security number, business or organization, and the manner in which you were prepared to pay for your purchases. More than 150 people signed for paddles.

The people with paddles looked at one another. They looked at each other's shoes and socks, watches and rings, belts, tie clips, bracelets and cuff links; they looked at coats and trousers, at the cut, the fabric, the weave; they looked for clues to prosperity. They looked each other up and down with discernment and disconcerting envy. Who would up the stake? Who would go one better? These people were going to war for the ruby slippers.

One young man dressed in shorts sat up front. Was he the one? Conversations carried and names were dropped. Who was there? Who was on the phone? Rumor had a paddle in Steven Spielberg's hand, hidden somewhere behind an anonymous face in the room. And Ted Turner sent his representative to "evaluate" the auction. He carried some company money, too.

The bank of telephones near the back of the room connected other far-away bidders to Christie's representatives, bidders from Great Britain to California, and around the Pacific Rim. At least a dozen of their representatives held phones to ears and paddles in hands.

Chip Baldoni, a used-car salesman from Long Beach, flew to New York for the occasion. In his wallet he had a $30,000 cashiers check made out to Christie's and another $10,000 in credit cards. "Having a paddle was a financial statement," he admitted, "but I was really hot to get the shoes. I thought with my 30 grand, plus credit cards, maybe I wouldn't get the shoes but I would be in the ball park. I was very excited."

Bill Thomas, my newfound source, went to New York with $50,000 in cash stuffed inside his black cowboy boots. "My dream was to buy the pair, so I would have two, and maybe someday, all the pairs of ruby slippers. I thought I had a chance," he said, "but when that man walked into the room, I said to my friend, 'that man is frightening. He's got energy.' I knew he would be the one to buy the shoes."

* * *

That day, Anthony wore a tweed sport coat with elbow patches, a smart pair of wool trousers and a plain, button-down shirt, open at the collar. His salt-and-pepper hair made him look like a young man going prematurely gray. But he was much older, a grandfather, in fact.

"For 50 years I've been a fan of Judy Garland," Anthony said. His New York accent was as thick as deli corned beef. "I'm only a collector of Judy Garland. I have photos, et cetera. As soon as I heard about the auction, I went directly to Christie's.

"When the ruby slippers were on display at Christie's, I was the first one there. My face was right up against the glass. You would think I was a child in a candy store. Right there I made up my mind: I was going to buy the shoes.

"I was there in person," Anthony said, "to make sure nothing went wrong. I was probably the first person there. I was going to be in charge."

* * *

The slippers were displayed on a podium under a plexiglass hood in the otherwise plain auction room. The auctioneer, Kathleen Guzman, presided over sales of costumes and textiles, bringing her gavel down once every minute. Lot #125 did not come up for sale until about noon.

"A kind of hush filled the room," Julie Collier said, "like when you take a deep breath. It was electrifying."

The auctioneer opened the bidding with a joke: "Do I hear fifty?" People laughed, and then the business began. "Do I hear $14,000?" she asked. Somebody piped up and it started. The bidding went up in increments of $2,000. Sixteen, eighteen, twenty, twenty-two, twenty-four, $26,000, then it hit thirty.

"It went so fast," Anthony said. "There were telephone bidders, there were representatives in the back of the room, all screaming."

Maybe screaming in the back of his mind. "There was no screaming at all," Julie said.

"It was so quiet, you could hear a pin drop," Chip Baldoni added. "When it hit thirty grand, the bidding jumped. Thirty-five, forty, forty-five, fifty — you didn't have time to converse, it went up so fast. It kept going up at five thousand increments to $100,000, and then it slowed down and you could breathe for five seconds. The auctioneer said 'It's only money.' She said 'how about 105' and someone on the telephone offered 110, then 115, 120. It came down to the guy in front wearing short pants and tennis shoes and a man in back wearing a grey suit."

* * *

"The bidding went up so fast," Anthony said with amazement. "My paddle went up and I never pulled it down. It hit one hundred thousand, one twenty, one twenty-five, one thirty, one thirty-five. I pulled my paddle down. I had to think. One forty-five.

"My four sons live in New York. I traveled into town with one of them that morning. In the car, he said, 'Go for it. Bring 'em home, Pop.' I heard that in my head. 'Bring 'em home, Pop.' That's when I threw my paddle back up. Onehundredandfiftythousanddollars... sold! I couldn't believe it."

There was an explosion of applause and hurrahs at the close of the sale. The room went nuts. Television cameras went into action and the press quickly closed in on Anthony. From his seat on the aisle, he rose and put a newspaper over his face. He ran into a little room. Reporters hovered, hoping for an interview.

"As soon as I purchased the shoes, I covered my face and ran out of the room. I ran right into the arms of the Christie's staff. 'Just get me out of here,' I said.

"We went up to the office and I had a cup of coffee. I was excited. Christie's wanted me to come down for a news conference. I told them I didn't want to, that I didn't want anyone to know my name. They said they'd have to say something to the reporters. What did I want to say about buying the slippers? I said I was going to treasure them."

* * *

The winning bid of $150,000 meant that Anthony would actually pay more than $178,000 to purchase the ruby slippers, including a 10% commission to Christie's and sales taxes. As a matter of record, which it was for the sale of any single item of Hollywood memorabilia, Christie's reported the official purchase price as $165,000.

Roberta Bauman was home in Memphis. At about 11 a.m. local time, Roberta received a call from Julie Collier.

"Hello, Mrs. Bauman," Julie said. "Are you all right?"

"Yes, fine."

"Are you sitting down?"

"Yes."

"In all of my 12 years here I have never experienced such a gathering, such an electric feeling, as at this auction. Each time the gavel went down there was murmuring and the mouths would fall open. When the gavel fell for the final time the price was $150,000!"

"A hundred and fifty thousand!" Roberta took a big gulp of southern summer air. "I never dreamed," she said. It took several days for the staggering figure to sink in.

* * *

Roberta called me after she finished speaking with Julie. "I feel very peaceful and calm now," she said. "Before the auction I was just kind of tightened up. The finale of the auction is the way I hoped it would end."

She called the man who bought the shoes "Mr. Wonder" because she wondered who he was. "I hope that Mr. Wonder will show the shoes to this generation of children and keep the story alive. I hope that he will in some way pick up where I left off."

I asked Roberta if she was a little bit sad about selling the slippers that had been in her family for half a century. "Why should I be sad?" she asked. "This is the happiest time in my life, but I didn't know I was going to get this happy!"

* * *

What Anthony did not immediately realize as he rushed out the door of Christie's was that he had purchased much more than a pair of ruby slippers. Roberta Bauman's shoe box contained fifty years worth of memories and friends. Soon, one by one, they would find their way to Anthony, look him over, like skeptical brothers checking out their baby sister's first date, and decide if he was "worthy" to hold Roberta's slippers — Dorothy's Shoes.

"Just because a man has a lot of money doesn't mean he has the right to own the shoes," Tod Machin said, immediately following the auction. Roberta distanced herself from this discussion by giving Anthony the benefit of the doubt, but she made clear her feelings.

Anthony took immediate possession of the slippers and prepared to return to his residence in Florida. "When I flew home, I put them in a small, very loose bag, and carried it on the plane. I put the bag in the overhead compartment, right above my head. Nobody was going to touch them."

The first few days he spent privately, sharing his new possession with only his family. Then he began to open up. He had been in touch with Julie Collier for obvious reasons and she relayed messages from Roberta, Tod and me. Roberta was the first to get a call.

Roberta told Anthony what it would mean if he called Tod. "This young man," she told Anthony, "is a part of my family." It was Tod he had to win over, but Anthony didn't know that. He called only because Roberta had asked him to, so quick was the personal bond between the seller and buyer.

Tod was immensely pleased. Tod and Anthony talked about Roberta, *The Wizard of Oz* and other intangibles shared by people under the spell of the slippers. After the conversation ended, Tod sat down and wrote a letter to Anthony.

"I must admit," he wrote, "when Roberta first approached me with the notion of parting with the slippers I was apprehensive. Not knowing who might buy them or what their future would be, I feared that their innocent magic might come to a halt. Now that all is said and done, I am thrilled to say that the magic lives on. I completely approve of you as their new keeper."

"I have a granddaughter," Anthony told me six months after the auction, "four years old. She is an *Oz* enthusiast already. I guess it's my fault, but she knows the movie word for word. When I showed her the ruby slippers, at first she was very frightened. She ran to the corner of the room. Then she got excited.

"Things run through your mind. Before I bought them, I had all these plans. I was going to display them in my home. But when I paid so much money — half a life's savings — I began to think. Now I can't even display them. I have to keep them in a bank vault.

"I feel I have taken on a tremendous responsibility. I don't really own them. The people own them. People should be able to see them. I cannot display them in my home; but I cannot keep them in a bank vault. They deserve to be seen."

* * *

What seemed to get lost in the tidal wave of publicity that flooded the sale of Roberta Bauman's ruby slippers was that Christie's, three weeks later, completed a private sale of another pair of ruby slippers; this time it was the Witch's Shoes.

On Tuesday, August 9, Christie's quietly announced that Philip Samuels of St. Louis had purchased, for $165,000, a pair of ruby slippers from an anonymous consignor. The shoes were marked "#7 Judy Garland." Instantly I knew what had happened and I could see how the story of the slippers would continue, so long as people pursued them.

Philip Samuels is the owner and founder of a fine art gallery that is a child's wonderland. He collects antique toys, particularly those made in America, and has effectively captured a dozen generations of adolescent fantasy in the name of a business which he thoroughly enjoys. To Philip Samuels, the ruby slippers were a natural reflection of his acquisitive taste. He set his mind upon them and found a way to get them, though quite by accident.

Samuels bid by phone for Roberta's slippers during the June auction. "I bid up to $110,000," he said. "That's where I stopped." Though he was not the under-bidder in the sale, he impressed Christie's officials with his sincere desire to own a pair of the slippers.

Upon completion of Roberta's successful sale, Kent Warner's prized pair of ruby slippers, size 5B, were offered to Christie's by the very same "anonymous" man who had purchased them for $12,000 in 1981.

The seller wanted to capitalize quickly on the fever that had reached an apparent crescendo with the sale of Roberta's shoes. But Christie's officials questioned the wisdom of offering a second pair of slippers for public sale within so short a time of the first. They didn't feel they could match the enthusiasm. It was decided to conduct a private auction among registered under-bidders and any other parties who learned of and were interested in the sale.

Thus, Philip Samuels and several other individuals submitted private bids. Samuels, based on the previous sale, figured the shoes would not sell for less than $150,000, and that's what he bid. Again, the under-bid was in the amount of $145,000, made by the same person who had been represented at the June auction by the man in the short pants and tennis shoes.

The quiet sale proved lucrative to all. The seller made ten times his investment in less than seven years; he actually made more money than Roberta, because he did not have to pay Christie's for any advertising or catalog production. (Roberta paid them close to $17,000, half the total cost of publicizing the sale of her shoes.) Christie's reaped a second commission and Philip Samuels had his slippers.

In terms of slippers entering the public eye, it was a wash, but a wash to the good side. While Roberta's shoes — Dorothy's Slippers — went from a public owner to an anonymous one, the Witch's Shoes came from private hands into public view. Philip Samuels would make the shoes available to the public. I had a feeling that Anthony would come around in his own quiet and dignified manner.

* * *

THE TROUBLE WITH WARNER BROTHERS

I wasn't surprised to learn that Bill Thomas had attended the Christie's auction. He was a familiar face around the New York auction houses. In 1984, Thomas took a number of famous movie costumes to Sotheby's for auction. His sale gained notoriety for publicly establishing the modern Hollywood memorabilia market. Thomas boasted of this achievement.

Indeed, the sale was a landmark of sorts. It told people that Hollywood memorabilia wasn't trash and opened the market to burgeoning profits and a wider clientele. But the sale was notorious for other reasons. Bill Thomas had a problem with The Burbank Studios.

Just as The Burbank Studios had attempted to prosecute John LeBold three years earlier, they came after Thomas, alleging that his auction included items that properly belonged to Warner Brothers.

Burbank Studios' officials were alerted to the December sale when they received the Sotheby's auction catalog in late summer of that year. A number of items in the catalog were Warner Brothers costumes. The red flag went up.

"They called just before five o'clock, the night before the auction, brought in the FBI and claimed that I was selling stolen property," Thomas told me. "I had to come up with a bill of sale for everything, on the spot, or the auction would not go on."

Thomas spent the night with representatives of the FBI, Sotheby's and lawyers for The Burbank Studios. When it was revealed that Sotheby's had mailed catalogs by registered mail to all the studios months before the scheduled auction, the question came up: Why hadn't The Burbank Studios acted sooner? The FBI immediately backed off the complaint.

Thomas eventually settled with The Burbank Studios by handing over some of the costumes from the auction, but he did so to avoid further litigation — months, maybe years of legal bills — rather than out of guilt. Charges were never pressed by TBS. Thomas knew they wouldn't be. He knew about previous efforts to prosecute John Le-Bold. He knew very well.

* * *

John LeBold didn't like talking about Bill Thomas. I could tell that by the way he fidgeted with his hands and how he moved his eyes. He talked like someone who'd been hurt.

Thomas and LeBold had met long before LeBold's troubles with Warner Brothers and The Burbank Studios. Their friendship went back to relationships with Kent Warner and Ron Wind.

"You can't imagine the emotional feeling," LeBold said. "My mother and I took Bill in and I totally trusted him when he was staying here. I was in trouble with Warner Brothers and there were a lot of costumes at my house. Bill said, 'Let me take care of them at my house, in case anything happens.' So many things have disappeared forever because of what Warner Brothers did to me.

"Bill had a playhouse in the backyard of his parents' home and he took a lot of my clothes and put them there under his mother and father's supervision. I totally trusted this boy. I'd known him for years."

Thomas agreed that he helped LeBold by storing hundreds of costumes that Warner Brothers might have confiscated. But the arrangement wasn't for just a couple of weeks; because of the lengthy court proceedings and ensuing trauma that affected LeBold's health, Thomas kept the costumes for nearly four years. It wasn't until LeBold made plans to open his own Hollywood memorabilia museum, in 1984, that he requested the return of the costumes.

"One day," LeBold said, "I asked for them back because the museum was about to open and he said, 'Oh.' The next day he comes over and looks at me like I was death. I said, 'What's the matter, what have I done?' and he said 'I hate you and don't want to ever see you again. Your costumes are going to be delivered. My mother and father are bringing them over.' The mother and father stormed into my house a few days later and brought like half the costumes back. I said 'Where's the rest?' and Bill said, 'They're all here.' I said, 'No, they're not,' and he came over to me and said, 'Well, give me two or three for payment for all the time you kept them at my house.' I said, 'Well, that's okay,' and he named two or three costumes and those were definitely missing. But a month later I got the catalog from Sotheby's with all the rest, about a hundred other costumes. Now that I've gone through an inventory of everything, I've realized that there's several hundred missing."

That's when LeBold said he discovered that his pair of ruby slippers was missing.

"The slippers were something that were hidden in my house and I didn't even know that he knew where they were," LeBold said, referring to Bill Thomas. "When I realized that the costumes were missing, that I wasn't getting them back and they were going up for sale at Sotheby's, I ran to where I had those things hidden and the slippers were gone."

* * *

Thomas flatly denied taking a pair of ruby slippers from John LeBold. "I don't believe he ever owned a pair," he said. "He did have the Arabian test pair, which Debbie owns, at his house for a while. I saw them. He told me they were his, but later he said they were Debbie's. That might be the pair he says were stolen." Thomas was calm about the question. He'd heard the accusation before. It was nothing new.

I asked about the costumes he had stored for LeBold, and he said everything was returned, with the exception of a few garments which the two men agreed upon as a storage payment. But how did Thomas explain his ownership of the costumes that sold at Sotheby's?

It usually takes about six months to arrange an auction with one of the major New York houses, especially in a field such as Hollywood memorabilia. Bill Thomas' auction at Sotheby's was in December, 1984, approximately six months after he and John LeBold had their blow-up.

"They were mine," he said. "I'd purchased most of them from people like Kent and Ron Wind."

It was the relationship with Ron Wind that triggered the worst feelings between Thomas and LeBold. They carried their feud over the bed of a dying man.

* * *

"Ronny and I were so close it was incredible," LeBold said. "He was like my best friend for life and I was supposedly his. We had even gone to a lawyer that was next door to his house, and I left my home and everything that I owned to him, and he left everything that he owned and his home to me, and many times during those last few years when he was sick I made all the payments for the house because he just couldn't do it anymore. He just couldn't get up. He hadn't worked for years."

"When Ronny was put in the hospital I traveled all the way down to Long Beach every day to see him and tried to take care of my mother here and him there, and I was sick, too. It was very hard on me. And when he came back home I went over to the house in the morning and at night. I bathed him and did everything for him...

"...Then one day, shortly after this whole Sotheby's thing had happened and I found out what kind of person Bill was, I walked over there and Bill was sitting there. I looked at Ronny and said, 'What is he doing there?' Ronny said, 'Oh, he's moving in, he's going to take care of me. You can't do this all the time.' I said, 'After what he did to me, you, my best friend, are letting him live with you? You won't have anything left in the house by morning.'

"I don't know what happened," he stated.

Even though we were talking on the phone I could sense LeBold shaking his head.

"I don't know what was said. But Ronny was definitely afraid of being left alone at night. Somebody had broken in one night while he was alone and had scared him half to death, a burglar, and he was terrified. But he was very helpless, and I could not leave my mother alone and stay with him. So we sort of quieted down our friendship for a while...

"...I called him almost every day, to be sure he was okay, but I couldn't be in the same house with Bill. One day, Ronny calls my mom. I was on the other line, and they were talking. So I was waiting to get on and he says to my mom, 'I know you and John are having terrible financial problems because of the museum, but you don't worry, I don't have very much longer. Know you have the house and everything I own, and pretty soon you guys will have it easier. All you have to do is sell the house and all the stuff.' Ronny was dead three weeks later."

Ron Wind, I learned at the Hall of Records, died of a self-inflicted gunshot wound to the head on March 22, 1986. Apparently, the dying man could no longer stand his pain. On his death certificate, no known relatives were listed; only the name of Bill Thomas appeared, as executor of Wind's estate.

* * *

The relationship between John LeBold, Bill Thomas and Ron Wind was an emotionally charged triangle, as difficult after Ron's death as it had been in his life. But from this relationship, Thomas charted the inner boundary of my search for the ruby slippers through the underworld of Hollywood memorabilia.

"We've been fighting among ourselves for years," Thomas said. "The irony of these fabulous gowns is that they are all fabulously tainted. But if not for the taint, they wouldn't even exist." And the taint was no more evident than with the ruby slippers.

Western Costume Co. on Melrose Avenue in Los Angeles, Ruby Slippers may have been made here.
Note open sixth floor window above the parking lot, where costume disappearances may have occurred.

Flyer advertising novelty shop owned by Ted Smith, who publicly boasted of owning a pair of Ruby Slippers. For the ad, Smith used a photo of the shoes from Christie's East.

Kent Warner as he prepared to deliver the Ruby Slippers to the MGM auction podium in 1970. Moments after this photo was taken, the shoes sold for $15,000 to an anonymous buyer.

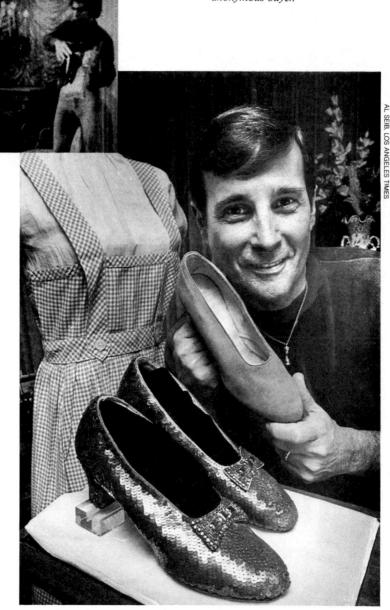

OZ collector Michael Shaw, seen with his pair of size 5½ Ruby Slippers, a Dorothy dress and a Ruby Slipper, sans sequins. Shaw obtained the slippers from Kent Warner.

Ron Wind, left, and Kent Warner peek over Judy Garland's shoulder at the Governor's Ball, following the Academy Awards ceremony on April 5, 1965.

Kent Warner and Ron Wind on the set of The Smothers Brothers Show *circa 1969. Both saved a remarkable number of Hollywood costumes from destruction.*

A rare 1939 lobby card from The Wizard of Oz. *In May, 1989, a similar card sold at auction for $2,700.*

1955 title card for re-release of The Wizard of Oz.

Western Costume shoe shop where Ruby Slippers were reportedly made for Judy Garland. In background is shoemaker Mauricio Osorio.

Commemorative pair of Ruby Slippers, constructed in October, 1988, for the 50th Anniversary of the release of The Wizard of Oz, *using Judy Garland's original last #150.*

Replicas of the Ruby Slippers, built by OZ fan Jack Townsend. Six pairs of these slippers were manufactured and sold by Townsend for $250 each.

The Witch's shoes, as photographed by Christie's East in 1981, prior to their sale.

Liza Minnelli managed to fill the shoes of her mother by following in her footsteps to stardom. Pictured here holding her "Ruby Slipper" award.

Shoe Brouhaha — A slipper here a slipper there — OZ alumni and friends are recipients of the "Ruby Slipper" award. (left to right) The Tin Man, Jack Haley; with son Jack Haley, Jr.; Liza Minnelli; The Wizard of Oz *producer Mervyn LeRoy; Munchkin Billy Curtis and Scarecrow Ray Bolger.*

Philip Samuels, who purchased the "Witch's shoes" in August, 1988 for $165,000 from Christie's East in a private auction that followed Roberta Bauman's successful June, 1988 sale.

The author visits Roberta Bauman's Ruby Slippers as displayed at the Beverly Hills Hotel prior to their sale by Christie's in June, 1988.

OZ fan Tod Machin, left, joins Munchkin Mickey Carroll to gaze at Ruby Slippers owned by Philip Samuels.

Philip Samuels and friends pay tribute to his new pair of Ruby Slippers at a gala party benefiting the "Make-A-Wish" Foundation in December, 1988.

The Ruby Slippers as photographed by the Smithsonian Institution.

The "Witch's shoes," as photographed by new owner Philip Samuels.

*"Dorothy's shoes" as displayed by their new owner, Anthony Landini, at the Disney/
MGM Studio theme park in Orlando, Florida.The shoes will be displayed there through 1994.*

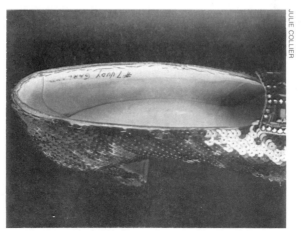

Close up of writing in the "Witch's shoes," reading "#7 Judy Garland."

Anthony Landini, left, and Roberta Bauman at the grand opening of the Disney / MGM Studio, where one pair of Ruby Slippers will be on display through 1994.

Close up of writing in Michael Shaw's "Traveling shoes."

*"Dorothy's shoes," as consigned by Roberta Bauman to Christie's East in the Spring of 1988.
These sold for $165,000 on June 21, 1988.*

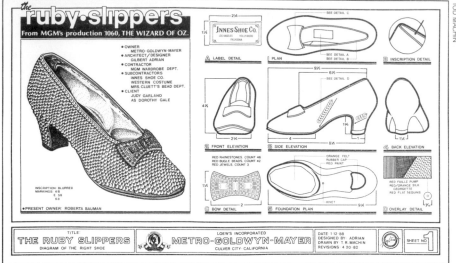

Architectural rendering of a Ruby Slipper, illustrated by Tod Machin.
For his model, Machin used "Dorothy's shoes."

"There's no place like home."

I asked Thomas about them again. Could I see them? Photograph them?

"It's a very personal thing for me," he replied. "I don't want the slippers photographed. I keep them in a safe deposit box. I would love to hold them again, but I won't see them until I deserve to see them."

"Until you 'deserve' to see them?" I repeated with disbelief. He answered yes, without emotion. He meant what he'd said.

His weird statement gave me cause to look deeper than the words. What was he saying? Was he a total flake, or was this some new wrinkle on sado-masochism? I had to ask: "Did you do something bad?"

"I think so," he said. "Yes. Yes, definitely, I think so. I think we all did something bad, and we talked about that a lot, and I made a very conscious effort at one point in my life to realize that we were just justifying wrongdoing, and that wasn't correct.

"So from that point on I've worked very earnestly to rectify that. And by that I mean doing everything upstanding, acquiring everything legally, paying taxes on things legally. Yes, I was a party to the wrongdoings that were being done in the name of history."

* * *

By Thanksgiving of 1988, I had been searching for ruby slippers for two years and still had found only four pairs to actually exist. If I were to believe Bill Thomas, then there were five, but he offered no confirmation. Furthermore, his odd statements seemed to epitomize the absurdity of my own obsession. And for what purpose? I had intruded on people's lives for something so fleeting and valueless as curiosity satisfaction.

The very nature of the saga of the slippers dictated that an end to the story was not forthcoming, not so long as there were slippers and people who desired them. The shoes would pass from hand to hand to hand, and the story would continue. The fates, it seemed, were weaving a gigantic tapestry that would never be finished, threading individual lives into the picture. But my role as the hunter had to end.

As the holidays approached, I could not be prepared for the coming turn of events. Julie Collier grew excited over some information she discovered. "There's something I must tell you," she said on the phone, "but I can't tell you just yet." It was obviously a matter of confidentiality.

This excitement was tempered by some sad news that I'd been expecting. For months I had been worrying about David, Kent's former roommate.

David had been extremely helpful in opening the floodgate of friends — the people who were living who knew Kent. It was David who decided the time was right to talk about Kent. "Why not," he'd said. "Kent was for the preservation of Hollywood." And talk he did.

I normally called David during the day, at his office, but one morning that fall, I was told that David was at home, sick. I'd call back, I said. They said he wouldn't be back in. Frightening. But I had followed this trail long enough to expect, and understand the worst.

I was able to reach David at home and we talked several times about this and that. Mostly, I just checked in with him. His voice had weakened, and it took him longer to formulate thoughts. I ached from his pain. On December 7, David passed away.

David left me with words I could not forget, the words he uttered when we first spoke, words that could have then told me his fate: "Life has taken strange turns." I never asked what he meant. He was a quiet, proud, private man.

* * *

While David chose not to reveal certain intimacies he shared with Kent, he did give the executor of his estate permission to provide me access to personal papers relating to Kent. This amounted to a birthday card, which Kent gave David on June 10, 1972. It read:

Dearest David,
    As a popular song of the '30s put it, "I'd beg for you,
I'd steal for you, I'd take stars out of the sky for you, if

that's not love, it will have to do — until the real thing comes along."
   Happy Birthday Beautiful
   Kent

Reading Kent's words heightened my awareness that so many lives had come and gone during just *my* search for the ruby slippers. Suddenly this clear talisman seemed to pronounce an anathema.

"I DO BELIEVE IN SPOOKS"

John LeBold and Bill Thomas, however close they had been to Kent Warner, and however involved each had become in the burgeoning black market of Hollywood memorabilia, did not know the whole truth behind the mystery of the ruby slippers. But their collective tale provided the clues I needed to determine what actually happened at the MGM auction in 1970. I began to analyze the half-truths.

Kent Warner had not collected televisions, radios, cigarette lighters and Hollywood costumes because he liked TVs, radios, lighters and clothes. He had collected to turn back the clock of his life to the 1930s. A man born out of time who found a way to reverse the process.

Kent Warner was not a collector or dealer of Hollywood memorabilia so much as he was a fan of an era, a style of living. He was devoted to Hollywood's golden age, the marvelously rich 1930s, when Ginger Rogers had danced long hours with Fred Astaire, when Louis B. Mayer had made Judy Garland the tortured darling of a nation, and when Adrian had dashed off magnificent sketches of costumes in a travel book while romancing the world Kent loved. Warner surrounded himself with these images from the past to support his image of his existence in that world.

Kent truly loved the movies of old Hollywood. He was a fan, a buff and a patron. He loved the Hollywood of fabulous song and romance, dashing heroes and sumptuous heroines. And he cherished the beauty of this image, cherished the beauty that others threw away. Quick words could not properly express Kent's anger when he found Hollywood treasures at the bottom of trash cans. His anger precipitated action. In these old clothes, cast aside by the studios, and tugged at by his friends, who grasped to control the destiny of costumes to the point of ripping them to shreds in vicious tug-of-war games, Kent found the ultimate paradox. Here, in all these costumes, were memories of the past. As simple garments, they dehumanized the myth. And myth is nothing if it cannot in some way maintain a mysterious legend.

Maybe Kent thought about telling the world what really happened with the ruby slippers, and then thought better of it. To tell the world might take the fun out of it. Why demystify the legend? Why take the ruby slippers and turn them into just another pair of shoes? Why chop off the Easter Bunny's ears, as Michael Shaw put it? Why not perpetuate the myth and the mystery, even if it meant deceit.

I had to think like Kent to get to the truth, and Kent delighted in telling half-truths. He let people believe what they wanted to assume. The story of the ruby slippers must have provided him with endless pleasure, as he dropped various bits and pieces of what actually happened into the tales he loved to tell. Now I had followed his tracks long enough to have heard all the stories and have all the pieces in my hand. It was time to tap three times and put the puzzle together.

* * *

When Kent told Richard Carroll, the supervisor of the MGM wardrobe auction, "Here are some shoes Judy Garland wore in *The Wizard of Oz*," he had spoken nothing but the truth. But he willingly let Carroll, David Weisz and the rest of the world assume that the shoes were unique, which was not true, as Roberta Bauman quickly proved.

Consistently, Warner dropped other pieces of the puzzle. To Michael Shaw, Kent sold a pair of ruby slippers that he said had belonged to a co-worker who didn't care so much about Hollywood memorabilia. Shaw said he didn't think there was another person, but he considered what Kent told Ken Maley and Don Ritchie not more than a year or two after selling Shaw the shoes. He told them he had been quietly blackmailed for a pair of the shoes. A pair went to a man Kent worked with, they said. And Judy Carroll recalled the man, but not his name. "He was one of the older men who worked with Kent, they were friendly." These stories fortified my belief that Kent had told them the truth about "hush slippers;" but, again, only half as much as he needed to tell.

The story Bill Thomas remembered was of an old MGM wardrobe woman who told her daughter, a wardrobe department employee, where the shoes were stored in the vast repository of dust-collecting costumes. In exchange for the information, Kent promised the daughter a pair of the shoes. And to Thomas, Kent described the building where the shoes were found; an old sound stage, a barn, a place missing a roof. At the time, I didn't think this story jibed with what Michael Shaw had told me — that Kent found the shoes on the third floor of Ladies Character Wardrobe. Another half-truth.

* * *

Several days before Christmas I received a letter in the mail, in a plain white envelope, addressed by hand, with a return address label. Inside were four scraps of paper. The first three were cutout paragraphs, as photocopied and snipped by the sender. The fourth scrap was a note: "Please be discreet." I put the pieces of copied cutouts together:

> When I found the Ruby Slippers at MGM there were (I think) 4 pairs. One pair auctioned for $15,000.00. I kept 1 pair and know not where the other 2 pair went. The three pair I didn't get were very well worn. My perfect pair were most likely the 'insert' (close-up) shoes which were only used when the camera was extremely [sic] close on the shoes. When a film is made, and the script calls for a camera angle featuring a particular item close up, that 'shot' is al-

most always made at a separate time from the regular shooting of a scene. Thusly; when in *The Wizard of Oz* Glinda tells Dorothy to click her heels and say 'There's no place like home, there's no place like home' and the camera is featuring the ruby Slippers (very close up) the most perfect (my pair) of the Slippers was used.

To the question 'wouldn't Judy Garland have to have walked in the Slippers (my pair) at some time or other?' the answer is not necessarily [*sic*]. If the inserts were shot later or on a separate stage (as is often done) Ms Garland would have been handed a perfect pair of Slippers right at the shooting site. This would have insured that fact that the Slippers were indeed kept perfect for their featured moment of glory. After the 'shot' they were taken away and boxed to insure their perfection. As a person having been involved with film costume for many years I know these all to be fact. I've gone through 'inserts' many, many times.

Film costume buffs to whom I have spoken over the years very much agree with this theory. But... rest asured [*sic*]... this is the real thing!

                    Reguards, [*sic*]
                    Kent (Warner)

* * *

Kent Warner was the type of fellow who held onto common knowledge for pleasure. Did he know the time? Yes, but you still had to ask again. He delighted in such games, and this playfulness brought laughter to those around him. It also exposed the dunces.

It took me two years to figure out that Ladies Character Wardrobe and Mr. Culver's Barn were not two separate places, but one and the same. Think like Kent. It was one old building called many different things. Did Kent consciously refer to it by varying names? I doubted it.

Mr. Culver's Barn had been on the MGM back lot longer than anyone could remember. It had been built, legend had it, by Culver City's founding father, a 19th-century suburban farmer. It had always been used as a gigantic garage for costumes.

For more than half a century, MGM wardrobe department personnel had used the place to store costumes that, in all likelihood, would never be used again. Lavish, exotic costumes made for specific, one-of-a-kind pictures, like *Zeigfeld Follies* and *The Wizard of Oz*. Costumes that caused costumers to say, "What are we going to do with this?" Costumes that were over-designed, heavily beaded, brightly dyed, flowing with feathers; costumes that served a particular moment of movie magic, and that was it. They were put in storage in the old barn and forgotten.

Years of Southern California weather had rotted the building and, by the time Kent Warner arrived, it was destined for immediate destruction. The auctioneers were given the task of clearing out Mr. Culver's Barn.

* * *

Throughout my search, I attempted to talk with any and every person I could find who had known Kent, especially those who were among his friends in 1970. Early on, the names of many costumers crossed my desk. People said they might know Kent. Some did, some didn't and some wouldn't say.

There was one fellow in particular, and older man, who had worked with Kent on *Camelot* at Warner Brothers in the late 1960s. At the time I first called he said, yes, he had known Kent but only very causally and for a short period of time. He said he was not a close friend. I let the conversation go at that, trusting what he said.

Months later, Bill Thomas mentioned this costumer's name and I relayed my earlier conversation with the man. He wasn't like a friend, Thomas said, "Kent thought of him as a father."

I made an excuse to call the man back and ask him some silly question about Kent and *Camelot*. I struck a nerve, and the man said he had known Kent better than he'd previously admitted. He wasn't sorry about that; he was mad. "I *was* old enough to be his father," he said.

This man had been Kent's mentor, had hired him for a number of jobs at Warner Brothers and elsewhere. He was responsible for helping the young man "who was like my son" get into the Designer's Union.

"He worked on a number of projects with me," the man said. *Camelot, Paint Your Wagon, Rich Man, Poor Man, Jaws*. A lot of people were jealous of Kent. He had tremendous talent. He could take rags and make wonderful costumes. He was the most clever person I've ever known at making a character out of rags."

"Do you know how Kent got the job with the MGM auction?" I asked.

"Yes, of course," the man said. "I hired him."

It wasn't long before we were talking specifically about ruby slippers and the auction.

"The auctioneers thought that the ruby slippers were second-hand shoes. They were ready to toss them out. They were total jerks. They had no conception of costumes, no idea of the worth. They were schlock merchants. They could have made millions. I was so shocked I just quit. I quit the job long before the auction.

"Kent Warner was a decent young man, a bit flamboyant. It's a crime he didn't live on. He collected things so he could share them with the world. Kent was a fan. He loved the slippers because of what they were. Kent's plan was to present the shoes to Liza Minnelli. It did not happen."

"How many shoes were there?" I asked.

"There were three pairs that were found. There may have been five or six. I was not surprised. Personally, I felt that one pair would bring thousands, but several would be worth nothing. I was shocked when they were sold. It was a lot bigger than what I thought it would be."

I pressed on with questions, which raised the man's temper. Suddenly, he declared, "You're not going to get the truth about the ruby slippers from anyone but me or Rikki Roberts and I'm not going to tell you and Lord knows where you'll find her."

The name registered quickly. Rikki Roberts was the woman I had met at the St. James's Club months earlier. I already knew how to find her. Immediately I relaxed the sharp tack and softened my questions. The man was angry because he thought I was doing a hatchet job on Kent. Maybe I was, but I didn't intend to.

"Kent was a marvelous person," the man said. "If anybody has anything bad to say about him, you look closely at that person. I'd like to know the name of anyone who has anything bad to say about Kent."

* * *

Rikki Roberts might have been hard to find had her husband not been such a name-dropper. I remembered that he talked about this star and that party, and when I wanted to come back to the club I should give him a call because the owner was a personal friend. To be honest, I couldn't have cared less, but I took his phone numbers — three of them — written on a scrap of paper and stuffed it in the pocket of my sport coat. Now that I needed the numbers, I felt lucky to find the scrap still pocketed. Within minutes I was talking to the "old wardrobe woman" of Kent Warner's stories, asking her blunt questions.

"It was very painful," Rikki Roberts remembered. "These costumes were my babies. I was head of the department at that time, and I knew all the women who through all the years had tended those costumes, and it was hell to spend four months just getting this stuff together in order for it to be sold. Things were going out of there so fast at the time."

There's no doubt Kent saw the MGM auction job as his way to salvage pieces of Hollywood's past. In his wildest dreams, he hoped to find the ruby slippers. "Where are they?" he asked everyone. He knew they had to be there and he would find them, even if he had to go through hundreds of thousands of costumes scattered in buildings and stages and lock-ups from decades past all over the lot.

The ray of sunlight probably wasn't there but Kent surely climbed into the rafters of the old building, climbed up rickety wooden ladders to perches high above the floor, to dangerous places in search of the slippers and other treasures. It was dirty, dusty and decayed, from decades of moisture, brittle heat and colonies of moths munching on the rich fabrics of Louis B. Mayer's finest costumes.

Three tiers of racks rose from the second floor of the building to the ceiling, an exaggerated height of twenty feet. The ladies of the wardrobe department preferred not to go up there, and they didn't. At Rikki's suggestion, Kent did.

When the shoes were found, the man who was like Kent's father and Rikki Roberts were the only people who knew. Quietly, the slippers were disposed of. The three of them decided that one pair of ruby slippers was worth much more to the public than several pairs. So Kent gave Richard Carroll just the one pair, and no reason to think that any others existed. Then the trio kept the rest. At least that's what I guessed.

I called the man back. "There were three pairs that were found," he specifically said. One pair went to the auction, one pair stayed with Kent, and one pair went to Rikki Roberts. That was it, he said. But Rikki said differently. She said another pair went to the man. That made four pairs.

Rikki claimed that her pair had been burglarized from her home, along with everything else she owned, back in the early 1970s. The man flatly stated, "I don't have a pair." The funny thing was I hadn't even asked. The half-truths came together.

* * *

"PAY NO ATTENTION TO THAT MAN
BEHIND THE CURTAIN"

In his memoirs of the Second World War, Winston Churchill wrote of the Australian Brigades that aided the Allied assault on the North African city of Bardia in January, 1941, a time when the war was still very much undecided: "They sang at that time the movie song they had brought with them from Australia which soon spread to Britain:

> *Have you heard of the wonderful wizard*
> *The wonderful Wizard of Oz,*
> *And he is a wonderful wizard*
> *If ever a wizard there was.*

"This tune," wrote Churchill, "always reminds me of these buoyant days."

Like no other movie which had come out of that golden era of Hollywood, *The Wizard of Oz* filled the heart with hope in a certain and pervasive fashion. It was a movie we all came to know. In many ways, this prairie fairy tale is so real that we incorporate its phrases into our daily lives and from them we extract positive meaning.

It is a story we are instantly familiar with, because it is a story that we have all shared at some point in our lives, whether from a trek to the package store or through the mountains of Nepal; we share this story about going home.

L. Frank Baum sat down to write a story for children when he dreamed *The Wizard of Oz*. Pure fantasy, some will say, but he borrowed that fantasy from everyday life, from children as well as adults, and there is nothing in his story that is not real. Not if you believe.

Like any good storyteller, Baum was careful to build the foundation of belief, and he did so with clear and powerful examples of human emotion. "There's no place like home" is very powerful, very real. And the magic of the ruby slippers could get you there.

* * *

If ever a Dorothy there was, Roberta Bauman is one. At the age of 16—Dorothy's age, and, not so coincidentally, Judy Garland's age—Roberta, with about as much chance as a cyclone has of picking up a farmhouse and dropping it in the Land of Oz, came into possession of a pair of enchanted shoes.

Most likely, Louis B. Mayer's army of publicists intended to give the Hollywood prize to a girl near Garland's age as part of a stunt to promote the movie. Like Dorothy, Roberta had no preconception of the value of the shoes. She simply cherished them. And, like Dorothy, Roberta did not ask for shoes, but accepted them, face value, as a gift.

In Baum's book, Dorothy thought the shoes "just the thing to take a long walk in, for they could not wear out." Though she did not wear her ruby pair, Roberta regarded them as a treasure for children that would not wear out.

Little did Dorothy know that, at her journey's end, she would learn the shoes held much greater charm; likewise, little did Roberta suspect that these ruby slippers would fetch $165,000 at a movie memorabilia auction in New York. She was flabbergasted. The money turned out to be Roberta's retirement nest egg.

Money alone was not the charm the slippers revealed to Roberta. As they had carried Dorothy, the shoes carried Roberta down her own Yellow Brick Road. Dorothy met friends along the way, and so did Roberta.

"There are people in my life I would have never known had it not been for my ruby red slippers," Roberta said. Indeed, more people than I have chronicled in these pages, are part of Roberta's ruby slipper family. Her story, like the story of the slippers and Judy Garland

and Kent Warner, is not all luck and happiness. There has been tragedy.

* * *

January 20, 1989 brought horrendous news. Kathleen Guzman, the newly appointed vice president of Christie's East in New York and the auctioneer who had presided over the sale of Roberta Bauman's ruby slippers, phoned to tell of the death of Julie Collier. The day before, Julie had been hit by a truck on the streets of New York while riding her bicycle to work. She was only 36 years old.

Roberta Bauman gave comfort to Tod Machin and me. In 1984, she had lost her own son to a car wreck — the same year Kent Warner passed away. A mother's grief is wider than the mightiest river and wiser than any prince or president. We must remember Julie, Roberta said, for what she gave to our lives, her eternal gift.

* * *

Julie's death punctuated the underlying tragedy of this storied search for the ruby slippers. In truth, I had not learned so much about these red sequined shoes as I had learned about people. People made these shoes important.

I looked at the pathetic nature of Ted Smith, the man in San Francisco who had so badly wanted a pair of ruby slippers that he had concocted an elaborate hoax, possibly to save face, or to come to own his own pair by some magic in which he profoundly believed. "I have their essence," he reminded me.

I stared into the eyes of Michael Shaw, a man who said "If I never owned another possession, I'd be happy." A man who desperately wanted me to believe that his slippers were bona fide. He reminded me, again and again, of his generosity, which he expressed by taking his ruby slippers on dozens of shopping mall tours. For a fee. I called his beloved pair the "Traveling Shoes."

Michael Shaw wanted me to believe that his slippers were the perfect pair and that the pair owned by Roberta Bauman had belonged to a stand-in. He consistently maintained this contention, which I found hard to comprehend.

He spoke of his own dream for a day when Hollywood might have its museum and he could "loan" his slippers, maybe in perpetuity, with a simple card reading: "From the collection of Michael Shaw". Beneath this smooth sincerity, I couldn't help but feel his insecurity.

I listened to the movie star. For all her talk, posture, position and acquisition, the Debbie Reynolds collection has yet to be seen. One cannot question her desire for a museum. Countless meetings, press conferences and lobbying behind the scenes documented her efforts to erect this shrine to Hollywood's history. There's no doubt of her commitment to such an effort — she's spent so much money on memorabilia — but I had to question her intentions.

For a few hundred dollars, Debbie Reynolds had purchased the "Arabian test shoes" from Kent Warner during the 1970s. In one of our three conversations the legendary actress said she would be happy to let me photograph the shoes. Arrangements were to be made through her personal assistant. But when push came to shove, Reynolds had changed her mind.

The excuse she gave was that the slippers could not be readily found, that they were packed away in some difficult spot to reach. This I found hard to believe. Certainly, these slippers were among the most precious items in her collection — designed by Adrian, worn by Judy Garland. If they were inaccessible or packed in some dark storage, I wondered if they were protected from deterioration? Were they receiving the best possible care? I assumed they were. But proper care demanded knowledge of their whereabouts and therefore I continued to ask why this woman, so publicly intent on collecting, would be so private with her treasure? Was she hoarding? Why not let these "Arabian" shoes be seen?

Something that Reynolds said during an interview really bothered me: "When I die, there'll be a terrific auction!" This ran counter to everything she said about a Hollywood museum but helped me understand why the Debbie Reynolds collection remained hidden from the public eye for so many years, and why she wouldn't let me photograph the "Arabian test shoes." Beyond altruism, these costumes from Hollywood's glamorous, glorious past were the root of obsession which Reynolds readily admitted: *"As long as people want to collect, they become passionate and any excuse is good enough... stealing, hiding it, borrowing it, permanently borrowing it... there is no approach to this collecting business."*

If anyone I met was obsessed with collecting it was John LeBold who for the better part of a decade was the curator of Debbie Reynolds' proposed museum. That was a weird concept to me, a curator for a museum that did not exist but LeBold justified his paycheck with research, inventory, storage, restoration and acquisition. With LeBold, acquisition was the key. LeBold handled her costumes as if they were his own which allowed the proliferation of some of his dreams.

I doubt that John LeBold ever owned a pair of ruby slippers, but he had many opportunities to see them and I think he came to believe at least one pair was, for a time, his. He told me that he often kept many of Debbie's costumes at his own home because there was no other place to store them, and for a while the "Arabian test shoes" were in his possession. Maybe this was the pair of ruby slippers he professed to own.

John LeBold was a sad character. His pale blue eyes reflected the look of a man who could only see the world through the lens of a movie camera. To John LeBold, the movies of Hollywood were everything, and he became completely absorbed in pursuing the dreams that even the movie makers could not see. It was as if LeBold could not be held accountable for his actions. He was that obsessed. And having these costumes became his ultimate spiritual release. Like wealthy men who can't get enough money, neither could LeBold get enough of this consuming passion. So LeBold made enemies.

And Bill Thomas reminded me of a memorabilia mercenary. He had long ago abandoned the idea of a Hollywood museum, though he preached the importance of preservation. In his mind, there was no guarantee that any of the players, including Debbie Reynolds, would ever realize the proper repository for so many historic Hollywood memories. Besides, so many of the costumes had already gone the way of the winds, through auctions and underground dealings.

Thomas believed in the auction process as the best way to find appreciative owners for the costumes that had been saved, and he was definitely part of this new wave of thinking. His auction at Sotheby's in 1984 was the first of its kind and spoke well for the future of entertainment memorabilia. He would continue to cash in, selling costumes acquired by whatever means.

He was also the only figure honest enough to say where these costumes had come from, how they carried a taint, and that if not for the taint, they wouldn't exist. "The reason that Hollywood costumes have become what they are is because of four or five people. Kent Warner, Ron Wind, John LeBold and Debbie Reynolds. And me. And the irony is that we're fighting to acquire garments worn by people who never existed. It's all fantasy, but to our world, it's very real."

* * *

As for Kent Warner, here was a figure I came to know only though memories. His passionate but tragically shortened life seemed to represent everything that ever was golden about Hollywood. Yet his desire to possess the slippers, and their charm, seemed to predicate eventual sorrow. Here was the irony. How could something so pure and simple as the ruby slippers be the source of so much grief? Kent's passion and his pursuit of the magical shoes epitomized their hold over people, yet it also characterized the inherent emptiness of people who too easily achieve their dreams.

But more than anyone else, Kent understood the importance of saving the ruby slippers and other costumes for history. And if not for Kent, these things might never have been saved.

* * *

"Glamor is my business," Kent told Kathleen Hendrix of the *Los Angeles Times* on the day she visited his home for an interview. "I live in fantasy constantly. But I'm a realist. I'm down to earth. I'm into the reality of doing, living, loving, cleaning the car, paying the bills... that's why today I'm probably less and less into fantasy and collecting and more into preservation.

"I just think that these things are beautiful. I've never been an outdoorsy person. I prefer man-made, wonderful things. If one believes in a God, aren't these things God-created too? Man was made by God."

And the myth of Dorothy's shoes was made by man. Kent told stories all right, and his story of finding the slippers would be hard to believe without the miracle of imagination:

"There was rack after rack of shoes. Everything was covered with dirt and cobwebs. It was hot, smelly, dark. It sounds so damned dramatic, but I swear it's true. A ray of sunlight picked up the glimmer of a sequin. 'Oh God, it can't be!' I walked over. I didn't touch them, I blew the dust from them, the red and the sequins appeared and I knew they were the ruby slippers."

"Why did you want them?" Hendrix asked.

"Why did I want them? Why did I want those damn shoes? I think *The Wizard of Oz* was the ultimate representation of home, family, solidarity, well-being, security — at the same time there was this madness and fantasy of *Oz*. All I can think of is the heels clicking and Judy saying, 'There's no place like home. There's no place like home.' "

* * *

Four pairs of ruby slippers are known to have survived the fifty years since the making of *The Wizard of Oz* at MGM in Culver City.

1.

DOROTHY'S SHOES

The first pair of ruby slippers to leave the MGM wardrobe department did so in 1939 when they were sent to New York for publicity purposes. They probably dressed the feet of a life-size Dorothy Doll, together with effigies of the Tin Woodman, Scarecrow and Cowardly Lion, as part of an MGM exhibition that promoted all the studio's movies. The effort may have been in concert with the 1939 World's Fair in that city. Following their promotional use, the size 6B slippers were awarded as a prize in a national "Name the Ten Best Movies of 1939" contest. Roberta Jeffries Bauman of Memphis, Tennessee, a high school junior, placed second in the contest and won the slippers, which were given to her on Tuesday, February 24, 1940. They were sent to Memphis and presented to Miss Jeffries in a plain shoe box.

The spool-heeled slippers are of red silk faille, covered with hand-sequined georgette and lined in white kid leather. Inside the right shoe is sewn a cloth label reading *Innes Shoe Co., Los Angeles, Hollywood, Pasadena*; also, the manufacturer's production numbers: E 58 68. The flat, jeweled bow is rimmed with 46 rhinestones, surrounding 42 bugle beads and three larger red jewels centered in a line; the stones and beads are imbedded on a bow-shaped piece of strap leather, an eighth inch thick and dyed red.

The leather soles are painted red and orange felt has been glued to the front foundation. A black rubber cap is on each heel. Their

The leather soles are painted red and orange felt has been glued to the front foundation. A black rubber cap is on each heel. Their condition is worn, with sequins missing, indicating substantial use during the making of the film.

In black ink, the word "Double" is handwritten on the white kid lining of each shoe; meaning these slippers were the second or third pair made for use in the production, in case the first pair were damaged or badly rent. "Double," as some have claimed, does not represent "stand-in" according to several MGM costumers familiar with the studio's practice of labeling wardrobe.

There is no question that stand-ins wore ruby slippers for lighting and blocking purposes, but there is no evidence whatsoever to support any claim that any pair of ruby slippers was worn exclusively by any stand-in. Further, there is substantial evidence to indicate that Judy Garland wore several different pairs of ruby slippers during six months of filming at MGM.

The slippers given Roberta Bauman were probably worn by Garland during many of the skipping and dancing scenes, judging from size and construction, including the addition of orange felt to the soles. They were probably the second pair of slippers to be built for use in the movie and were worn frequently, but not worn out.

These shoes have the clearest provenance of any known pair of ruby slippers and therefore provide collectors and historians the standard by which authenticity of other pairs appearing on the market must be measured.

The slippers remained the property of Roberta Bauman for 48 years, during which time she exhibited them solely for the benefit of children. She did not measure their value monetarily until June 21, 1988, when they were offered for public auction by Christie's East and brought $165,000.

On April 29, 1989, the shoes reappeared in the public eye at Walt Disney World in Florida, where they will be on exhibit for a period of five years. The loan was proposed to Disney by the new owner who agreed to reveal his identity. The reason he made the shoes available to the public, Anthony Landini stated, was because "the slippers deserve to be seen by children."

2.

THE PEOPLE'S SHOES

Currently on perpetual display at the Smithsonian Institution's National Museum of American History, these size 5C ruby slippers were presumably auctioned by the David Weisz Co. on Sunday, May 17, 1970 for $15,000. The anonymous buyer, represented by attorney Richard Wonder of Newport Beach, California, is considered by Smithsonian officials "to be the only link between the museum and MGM." The shoes were donated to the Smithsonian in December, 1979 and have since been on exhibit.

The uppers and heels are covered with red silk faille and overlaid with hand-sequined georgette. The leather soles are painted red, with orange felt adhered to front foundation. A black rubber cap is on the heel of the right shoe but missing on the left. The bow of the right shoe has 43 rhinestones surrounding bugle beads and three large red stones in the center; the left bow has 41 rhinestones surrounding bugle beads and three large stones. Rhinestones are missing on both bows.

Inside the right slipper is an embossed label reading *Innes Shoe Co. Los Angeles, Pasadena, Hollywood.* The color has been worn from the label. On the white kid lining of the right shoe, the manufacturer's number has been stamped 5BC 15250; on the lining of the left shoes, the number is 5C 11869 D536.

The condition of the Smithsonian slippers is poor, relative to other known pairs, suggesting that they were the first and primary pair of shoes made for and worn by Judy Garland during the making of *The Wizard of Oz*. They were probably worn more than any other pair known to exist, most likely during dance scenes along the Yellow Brick Road.

While the buyer of the ruby slippers at MGM in 1970 and the donor of the slippers to the Smithsonian remain anonymous, it is assumed that they are one and the same, thus establishing somewhat clear provenance of the shoes. However, these were definitely handled by costumer Kent Warner and must bear some consideration of his mysterious legacy.

3.

THE TRAVELING SHOES

Owned by Michael Shaw of North Hollywood, California, this pair of size 5 1/2 ruby slippers have often been mistaken for several different pairs of the shoes. During the 1980s, Shaw displayed his shoes at more than 25 shopping malls around the country. Further, this pair was exhibited in a privately owned movie memorabilia museum in Hollywood, and occasionally dressed the windows of several small stores in the Los Angeles area.

The slippers are in very good condition, but are also darker in color than any other known pair — a rich burgundy — suggesting they might have been used for static and close-up shots. However, the leather soles are covered with orange felt, eliminating the possibility that they were worn by Judy Garland during extra-close-up shots.

The red silk faille uppers and heels are covered with hand-sequined georgette, the leather soles are painted red, with the orange felt adhered to the front foundation of each shoe. The bows are perfect, missing no rhinestones, bugle beads or center jewels. Inside the right shoe is the label, embossed in silver, reading *Innes Shoe Co. Los Angeles, Pasadena and Hollywood,* and inscribed on the white kid lining is the name *Judy Garland,* written neatly with black ink in block letters. Manufacturer's numbers in the left shoe are 5BC 15250; in the right shoe they are 5C 11869 D536. The rubber cap on each heel has been painted red.

While not perfectly clear, the provenance of these shoes has been settled since 1970, when Michael Shaw privately purchased the slippers from Kent Warner for, reportedly, $2,500. That Warner handled the shoes must arouse the curiosity of collectors.

During 1989, the 50th anniversary of the release of the movie, these slippers traveled to Grand Rapids, Minnesota, Judy Garland's birthplace, where they were exhibited for fans who gathered to celebrate the star's 67th birthday. The shoes continue to be offered for public display at venues around the country and remain the private property of Michael Shaw.

4.

THE WITCH'S SHOES

These are Kent Warner's prized size 5B ruby slippers, which he found at MGM before the spring of 1970 and kept in his personal possession for more than a decade. They are distinguished from other pairs of ruby slippers by their size — smaller than others — and the lack of orange felt on the soles of each shoe, suggesting they are the pair of close-up or "insert" sippers worn by Judy Garland when character Dorothy taps her heels together three times in the movie's climactic scene. Kent Warner certainly believed this.

The red silk faille uppers and heels are covered with hand-sequined georgette and the shoes are lined in white kid leather. In the right shoe the embossed label is in gold and reads *Innes Shoe Co. Los Angeles, Pasadena, Hollywood.* Inscribed on the lining is *#7 Judy Garland,* written in block-lettered, black ink. The manufacturer's number written into the right shoe is X 68 02, 5B D 536. These shoes are in excellent condition, suggesting little wear, if any.

Of all the ruby slippers, the provenance of this pair is most mysterious. They were found by Kent Warner prior to the 1970 MGM auction and spirited from the studio without the knowledge of the auctioneers. For years, few people even knew of their existence. Warner publicly acknowledged possession of the slippers in 1977. His first attempt to sell them came in December, 1980, when they were offered at a movie memorabilia auction held at the Ambassador

Hotel in Los Angeles. Warner set a reserve of $20,000 and did not receive that bid. Later, Warner consigned the shoes to public auction at Christie's East, where they sold for $12,000 on October 1, 1981 to an anonymous buyer from northern California. On August 9, 1988, the buyer offered the shoes for sale at Christie's in a privately arranged auction that matched sealed bids and for $165,000 they were purchased by Philip Samuels of St. Louis, Missouri.

There is no way to know if Kent Warner altered this pair of ruby slippers in any way. Did he find "circular scuff marks" on their soles, or did he put them there; were they really the seventh pair of slippers or did he write #7 *Judy Garland* in them? Again, these questions have no answers. A date-test on the ink might be revealing.

The shoes are currently open to public view on select occasions at the Philip Samuels Gallery in St. Louis.

* * *

Several other pairs of slippers built for the production may still exist.

A.

THE ARABIAN TEST SHOES

These shoes were elaborately designed by Adrian, but do not appear in the film. They have been seen only in test shots, photographed in October, 1938. These shoes are owned by Debbie Reynolds who purchased them from Kent Warner for, reportedly, $300. Repeated requests to Ms. Reynolds for updated photos were refused so their existence can only be confirmed, but not documented.

B.

BUGLE BEAD SHOES

Allegedly found by Kent Warner, this test pair may have been worn by Judy Garland during director Richard Thorpe's two weeks of filming in October, 1938. They did not have bows. These shoes have yet to publicly surface.

* * *

One remaining pair of shoes are said to exist in the collection of Bill Thomas. According to him these slippers are size 5 and have Judy Garland's name written in the lining. Thomas refused to produce this pair for inclusion in this work.

* * *

While preparing this appendix, a remarkable revelation appeared in the form of the peculiar manufacturers' numbers that are written inside every pair of ruby slippers. As I gathered these numbers for publication, I noticed that none of them matched—none until Michael Shaw gave me the numbers for his shoes. I couldn't have imagined this:

The numbers in the right shoe of the pair owned by Shaw—5C 11869 D536—matched the numbers in the left shoe owned by the Smithsonian Institution! And, Shaw's left shoe—numbered 5BC 15250—matched the Smithsonian's right shoe!

What does not match are the sequined overlays. The Smithsonian overlays are rough and worn; Shaw's overlays are in perfect condition. This clearly suggests that the shoes themselves were mixed and matched before the sequined overlays were attached! Though the shoes are basically the same size, they are nonetheless subtly different, meaning that Judy Garland wore a wider shoe on her left foot than she did on her right for production of the movie.

This also lends credence to the theory that the basic ruby slipper—the French-heeled pump—was purchased in quantity by either Western Costume or MGM, depending who you believe made the shoes, and the sequined overlays were added somewhat haphazardly with regard to matched pairs. This revelation tends to support Harmetz' claim that the shoes were, in fact, made by MGM.

But what is more remarkable is the understanding how each surviving pair was used in the movie. Shaw's pair were obviously not worn as much as the Smithsonian pair, leaving one to surmise that his were "doubles," or extras, to be used in case the primary pair was damaged.

What cannot be explained is why the two other known pairs have no matching numbers between them. This supports the contention that there are more pairs of ruby slippers!

*** * ***

APPENDIX 2

MOVIE MEMORABILIA MARKET

ITEM	PRICES PAID
Ruby Slippers	$165,000
Chaplin Hat, Cane, Floppy Shoes	150,000
Casablanca Piano	154,000
Wicked Witch's Hat	33,000
Citizen Kane's Rosebud	60,000
Marilyn Monroe Blouse from *Bus Stop*	12,000
Judy Garland's Gown from *Meet Me In St. Louis*	2,750
Garland's Gingham Dress from *The Wizard of Oz*	22,000
Chaplin's *Great Dictator* Suit	3,850
Clark Gable's Jacket from *Gone With The Wind*	6,000
Clark Gable's Vest from *Gone With The Wind*	3,750
Adam West's *Batman* Outfit	8,500
Charles Middleton's *Flash Gordon* Outfit	14,300
Arnold Schwartzenegger Coat from *Terminator*	1,600
Robert Redford's Pants from *Butch Cassidy*	600
Debbie Reynolds' Dress from *How The West Was Won*	125
Garland's Hat from *Presenting Lily Mars*	1,300
Joan Collins' Dress from *Virgin Queen*	650
Vivien Leigh's Dress from *That Hamilton Woman*	3,500
Jack Lemmon's Dress from *Some Like It Hot*	1,700

Garland's Slip from *Easter Parade*	550
Jean Harlow's Gown from *Libeled Lady*	6,800
Mae West's Gown from *Every Day's A Holiday*	10,000
Douglas Fairbanks, Sr.'s Rags from *Robinson Crusoe*	550
Julie Andrews' Pinafore from *Sound of Music*	6,600
Errol Flynn's Outfit from *Adventures of Don Juan*	2,750
Keir Dullea's Flight Suit from *2001*	1,700
Vivien Leigh's Coach Gown from *Gone With The Wind*	16,500

ESTIMATED VALUE OF OTHER PIECES

Viven Leigh's Drapery Dress from *Gone With the Wind*	$150,000
Marilyn Monroe's "Diamonds Are A Girl's Best Friend" Dress from *Let's Make Love*	50,000
Monroe's Beaded Leather Leotard From *Gentlemen Prefer Blonds*	25,000
Monroe's Gold Lame' dress from the same	25,000
The "Tiger" Dress from *Seven Year Itch*	100,000
Monroe Dress from *Prince And The Showgirl*	20,000
Bogart Black Pinstripe Suit from *Maltese Falcon*	10,000
Rita Hayworth's "Gilda" Dress	50,000
Greta Garbo's *Queen Christina* Gown	25,000
Mary Pickford's Dress, *Taming Of The Shrew*	3,000
Rudolph Valentino's "Suit of Lights" from *Blood And Sand*	100,000
Marilyn Monroe's "Subway Dress" from *Seven Year Itch*	150,000

BIBLIOGRAPHY

$\mathbf{P}$rimary sources for this book consisted of interviews by the author with individuals related to the story. Many provided personal papers and correspondence. However, a body of published and publicly available literature supported the research.

Articles:

"L. Frank Baum Dead" *NEW YORK TIMES,* May 8, 1919.

"The Screen In Review" by Frank S. Nugent, *NEW YORK TIMES*, August 18, 1939

"Adrian, Designer is Dead on Coast" *NEW YORK TIMES,* September 14, 1949

"Judy Garland: Her Triumphs and Her Tragedies" by Vernon Scott, *UNITED PRESS INTERNATIONAL,* June 7, 1968

"Judy Garland Dies In London" *DAILY VARIETY*, June 23, 1969

"Judy Garland, 47, Found Dead" *NEW YORK TIMES,* June 23, 1969

"Judy Garland: Loneliness and Loss" by Vincent Canby, *NEW YORK TIMES,* June 29, 1969

"Tatters of an Empire" *THE TIMES SATURDAY REVIEW,* May 2, 1970

"Liz' Gown Nets $625" by the Associated Press, *LOS ANGELES HERALD-EXAMINER,* May 18, 1970

"$15,000 For Judy's Slippers" by United Press International, *LOS ANGELES HERALD-EXAMINER,* May 18, 1970

"Ruby Slippers From *'Wizard of Oz'* Bring $15,000 Bid" U.P.I., *MEMPHIS PRESS-SCIMITAR, May 18, 1970*

"Memphian Finds Mystery in 'Magic Red Shoes' " by Dorothy Y. Ward, *MEMPHIS PRESS-SCIMITAR, May 20, 1970*

"Mystery Arises Over Judy's Ruby Slippers" by William Endicott, *LOS ANGELES TIMES,* May 21, 1970

"Antiques 'Memories' For Orange Couple" by Larry LaRue, *ORANGE COUNTY REGISTER,* October 16, 1975

"One Man's 'Oz' and Ends: 'I discovered the Ruby Slippers' " by Kathleen Hendrix, *LOS ANGELES TIMES,* January 26, 1977

"Judy Garland's Treasures On the Auction Block" by Suzy Knickerbocker, *SAN FRANCISCO CHRONICLE,* November 4, 1978

"Kent's Room Has 11 Views" *TV GUIDE,* June 9, 1979

"Memphis Slipper Mystery Still Clicking" by David James, *THE SOU'WESTER,* October 31, 1980

" 'He Could Sell Anything' — and He Did" by Jeff Glass, *LOS ANGELES TIMES,* July 6, 1981

"Friends of Dorothy?" Author and publication unknown, September 1981

"Red Shoes From 'Oz' Bought for $12,000" by the Associated Press, *SAN FRANCISCO CHRONICLE,* October 21, 1981

"The Magical Shop of Mirth" by Stephanie Salter, *SAN FRANCISCO EXAMINER,* August 10, 1984

"A Sign of Hard Times: 'Oz' Ruby Slippers Must Go" by Randy Shilts, *SAN FRANCISCO CHRONICLE,* April 13, 1984

"Hollywood Museum Ready for Opening Next Monday" *LOS ANGELES TIMES,* May 14, 1984

"Gown of the Stars Modeled" by Benjamin Epstein, *LOS ANGELES TIMES,* October 5, 1984

"Oh Toto! 'Oz Slippers Stolen' *ASSOCIATED PRESS,* October 17, 1984

" 'Oz' Slippers in Wicked Hands" by Birney Jarvis, *SAN FRAN-CISCO CHRONICLE*, October 17, 1984

"Stolen Shoes" *UNITED PRESS INTERNATIONAL*, October 19, 1984

"Hollywood Museum Files for Bankruptcy" by Stephen Braum, *LOS ANGELES TIMES*, July 11, 1985

"Only One of All Our Millions" by John Fricke, *BAUM BUGLE*, Autumn, 1986

"Celebrity Clothing at Center of Battle" *ASSOCIATED PRESS*, June 8, 1988

"Hollywood Memories" by Pat Hilton, *FRANKLIN MINT AL-MANAC*, Franklin Center, Pa., November-December, 1988

Books:

THE WIZARD OF OZ, by L. Frank Baum, 1900, Ballantine Books, New York, 1979

THE MAKING OF THE WIZARD OF OZ, by Aljean Harmetz, A.A. Knopf, New York 1977. Limelight Edition, 1984

DEBBIE: MY LIFE, by Debbie Reynolds, William Morrow, New York, 1988

THE WIZARD OF OZ: THE OFFICIAL 50th ANNIVER-SARY PICTORIAL HISTORY, BY John Fricke, Jay Scarfone, William Stillman, Warner Books, New York, 1989

THE MUNCHKINS REMEMBER, by Stephen Cox, E.P. Dutton, New York, 1989

* * *

Those interested in pursuing the political parable of *Oz* will want to refer to the following articles:

"The Wizard of Oz: Parable on Populism" by Henry M. Littlefield, *AMERICAN QUARTERLY*, 1964

"The Wonderful Wizard Lives On" by Michael A. Genovese, *LOS ANGELES TIMES*, March 12, 1988

Books:
THE WIZARD OF OZ AND WHO HE WAS, by Martin Gardiner and Russel B. Nye, East Lansing, Michigan, 1957
TO PLEASE A CHILD, by Frank J. Baum and Russel MacFall, 1961
"What's the Matter With Kansas" by William Allen White, *GREAT ISSUES IN AMERICAN HISTORY,* Richard Hofstadter, ed. Vintage Books, New York, 1958
"The Boy Orator of the Platte" by John Dos Passos, *THE 42nd PARALLEL*, Houghton Mifflin and Co., Boston, 1930

* * *

Supplemental literature:
THE LETTERS OF F. SCOTT FITZGERALD, by Andrew Turnbull, ed. The Bodley Head Ltd., London, 1963
THE CORRESPONDENCE OF F. SCOTT FITZGERALD, by Matthew J. Bruccoli and Margaret M. Duggan, Eds. Random House, New York, 1980
THEIR FINEST HOUR, by Winston Churchill, Houghton Mifflin Co., Boston, 1949

* * *

Letters from David Weisz, Richard Carroll, Susan Schreiber, Julie Collier and Tod Machin's 1982 thesis titled *The Ruby Slippers* can be examined by request at the Smithsonian Institution's Division of Community Life.

37107